Faith
To Walk

Jen Johnson

When we believe something so strongly it moves us to act, a new gift starts to grow. The Gift of Faith.

CONTENTS

INTRODUCTION

Welcome friends.

I'm so glad you're here.

What if we were sitting together over hot cocoa or curled up on a couch?

This introduction would be a warm handshake, a shared smile, a gentle hug, or the quiet settling-in that comes with familiar company.

You're not about to read a manual on faith written by a scholar or an expert. You won't find formulas for holiness or instructions for flawless living in these pages.

Instead, what I have for you is simple: a collection of reflections, stories, and shared moments that capture the journey of faith as I've come to know it —full of questions, little discoveries, and the ongoing search for connection with God in everyday life.

Each chapter is shaped by experiences, conversations, and the gentle promptings I've felt from God. It's raw, honest, and as close as I can come to simply "talking" to you.

If you've ever stumbled in the dark, felt a nudge to take a leap you weren't sure you were ready for, or wondered if you're doing any of it right—this book is for you.

It's for the wanderers, the wonderers, the ones who feel their faith in the background of their lives, like a gentle hum that becomes more insistent with time.

It's for those of us who are constantly learning how to trust, who might be quick to question but are drawn back to faith by a steady hand that we sometimes recognize only in hindsight.

It's also for the steady plodders, the dutiful sorts. The erratic sprinters and the couch sitters. It's for all of us.

As we walk through these reflections together, you'll hear about times when I felt steady and sure, times when I was completely out of my depth, and times when faith felt more like a question than an answer.

Faith, I've come to see, is a journey that evolves

over a lifetime—sometimes slowly, sometimes with urgency, but always with purpose.

The journey of faith isn't about perfection; it's about movement.

It's about the faith to keep going, even when we can't see what's next. It's about stepping out into the unknown, learning to see the beauty in what we don't yet understand, and trusting in God's goodness and grace to guide us through each step.

An Every-day Kind of Faith

Faith isn't a feeling reserved only for mountaintop experiences or quiet moments of prayer.

It shows up in the everyday: in work, in family life, in laughter and struggle, in worry and relief.

Faith acts in every mundane detail of our lives, asking us to trust that something bigger than ourselves is at work, even when we can't see it clearly.

Times of uncertainty, worry, and darkness spur great moments of faith and trust.

In those moments, I look back and see that I didn't need perfect answers;

I needed faith—the faith to take one step forward, then another, and another, trusting that the path would reveal itself.

This book is an invitation to lean into that kind of faith—the faith to trust God's presence in our lives, the faith to believe that His grace is enough, and the faith to keep going every day in the little things even when we're unsure of what lies ahead.

A Conversation

This book isn't just about sharing my experiences; it's about sparking yours.

I hope these reflections remind you of moments in your own life where faith has carried you, or where you've felt close to something divine and beautiful.

I hope it encourages you to pause, think, and maybe even reach out to me to share what's on your heart.

http://www.jengeiglejohnson.com

My journey is different from yours, but in sharing our stories, we find the threads that connect us.

So, as you read, treat this book like a conversation.

Let it be a space where you can pause, reflect, and bring your own experiences to the table. Write them down. How would you respond to what you're reading? What would you say? Write it down.

Let it be a reminder that we're all navigating the same questions, the same doubts, and the same hopes.

This isn't about getting things "right" but about learning to live with grace, patience, and courage along the way.

It's about trusting the process and what it brings.

An Invitation to Walk Together

This book is my invitation to you—to walk with me, to explore the edges of faith, and to find God in the everyday spaces of life. I hope these reflections remind you that faith isn't about having all the answers or being certain all the time. It's about showing up, about trying and sometimes failing, about asking questions and holding onto hope. It's about becoming, slowly and imperfectly, the people God has created us to be.

And every step, however small, is an act of faith.

1

THE FAITH TO WALK

I stood at the top of a hill on the outskirts of a small village in Brazil. We were visiting families, and it was getting late so we turned down the path to go home.

Within moments, all the lights in the area went out.

During the time it took for my eyes to adjust to the new darkness, before a single star or the moon or even my hand in front of my face was visible, I thought about panicking.

But instead, I paused.

And I might have closed my eyes. I don't know because it would have made no difference in my ability to see anything.

I clutched my companion at my side. I didn't know how to get home in the dark. I didn't know what was on the ground in front of us or where my feet would step, where a path home started or ended or turned. I didn't know the area very well.

But immediately into my mind, I remembered what I did know.

I believed in God's power to help.

I believed in angels from Heaven.

I knew God heard my prayers.

It was as if my memories, the power of my faith in those very things, came to me right when I needed the reminder.

Has that ever happened to you? You remembered you have faith?

One thing God does for me often is help me remember things. It's a promise in the scriptures that the Holy Ghost can bring things back to the front of our minds.

And in this moment, He was also helping my faith to be strong enough to receive an important blessing.

I grabbed my companion's hands and held them close. "Let's pray."

I then prayed with surety, with faith, that God would be with us, that He would send his angels to walk with us in our front and at our sides and behind us to keep us safe and to help us find our way. (DC 84:88)

And He did.

I felt "encircled about" all the way home.

Sometimes we need an immediate rescue. And in our almost panic or full-blown fear, we need to find the faith to ask for what we most desperately need.

Grace is extended to us in these moments just like in response to the father in the Bible in Mark who said, "Lord I believe; help thou my unbelief." (Mark 9:24)

Sometimes in the New Testament, Jesus was found healing blind men by putting clay in their eyes. Or spitting in them. Or he healed the servant of Naaman by telling him to bathe in the dirty river. He let the apostles touch and feel his hands and feet after He was resurrected.

He helps our faith to grow. He does what He can to ignite the faith we need. This filling in where we need a little boost is a beautiful evidence of His Grace.

Grace is a power and a gift.

It is mercy and it is enabling.

It's strengthening and healing.

Grace is acceptance where we are and through

Christ's sacrifice, help to become who we need to be.

Jesus helps us to move, to work, to progress, to walk.

The faith to walk.

We need to be walking. Life is about doing, and God loves effort.

But sometimes we are standing in the dark.

Sometimes we are at the edge of what we think might be a cliff. We can't see the path ahead.

And we need to take that first step. But we are unsure.

These moments in life come all the time. I think I felt them more powerfully when I was younger. My decision to serve a mission for eighteen months in Brazil felt like a faith walk. Choosing to marry my husband, starting our family, moving far away, all of these things felt like an adventure, but they also felt a lot like the first of many steps of faith.

My son's club feet and treatment plans, my daughter's kidney trouble, ear infections in the middle of the night, decisions, so many decisions with not enough information or expertise to make them.

Choosing friends, opening up to others, social situations, business opportunities, becoming an author, working with others on committees, serving on boards, helping in the community.

And more. Walking with Faith is a daily choice, much more than I realized years ago.

It's often the small things. But sometimes big things come along too.

One time, I was waiting for my husband to come home from work and it was late, really late. I'd put all the kids to bed by myself after having played with them all day. I fed them, bathed them, read scriptures to them all alone. I was tired. And I wondered if I'd be doing everything alone like that a lot.

I started an Internet search looking for a place to live among the cities that I had heard had a more family friendly work schedule.

I immediately thought of Dallas even though I had no connections there at all. And in my first Google search of Dallas real estate, a certain town popped up.

I was flooded with a sudden feeling of love and comfort and energy, and I knew there was something special about this particular town.

I dug a little deeper, and the feelings continued.

I paused my search and prayed. "Do you want us to move to Texas?" My mind and heart were flooded anew with feelings and what felt like an assurance that we should do just that.

But moving four children to a completely unknown place, asking my husband to find a new job, selling our home and starting over...that was a walk of faith, based solely on the impressions I had that I knew were from God.

Was this one town simply one of many good choices we could make? Could we also stay in Virginia and be happy there? If I prayed about every city would I get the same response? What about timing? How soon should we move? Many questions could have clouded my reasoning. But I focused on what I knew, and that was simple. God had told me moving to Texas was a good idea.

My husband prayed about it. He agreed.

And so we did.

What happened? Was it everything I had hoped?

Yes and no.

It was definitely where we were supposed to live.

And we were so blessed to be there.

But there were also many times I turned back to remember the inspiration I had received and reminded myself that I had felt like the Lord was sending us there. The remembrance of those feelings fueled my faith and kept me going when things were tough.

We know God can help us remember and help grow our faith. But it's all about moving forward. It's all about the walk. We have to act.

And sometimes that walk involves a step into the darkness. It requires movement before knowledge. We get a spark, and that is enough to carry us into action. Then more knowledge comes.

In these instances, I can only say, fly. Fly as high as you can. You can do it.

These seemingly risky steps often become major hinge points in our lives and serve to launch us into greater paths and directions and experiences than we could have ever dreamed. If you're sitting on a precipice and you suspect it would be a wonderful move, be brave, take the leap.

With prayer, with the spirit, with God's grace.

Acting, moving, walking, will make all the difference.

A little forward motion and your faith will grow which will move you to act some more, walk some more, and again your faith will grow.

The Faith to Walk is about all the times in our lives that require us to move forward not totally seeing, not having perfect knowledge, but hoping, desiring, and acting on what we do have. The more

I think about it, the more I'm convinced that recognizing and cultivating this kind of faith is the most important thing we can do.

Whether you have a tiny sliver of unpracticed faith or a lifetime of growth and proof, the more we act, the more we will grow. The faith to walk is about the acting, the walking, and the doing.

2

PETER WALKED AND STARTED TO SINK

Peter didn't just *hope* he could walk on water.

He actually walked on water.

He stepped out of the boat and took steps on top of the water, during a storm.

Wind.

Waves.

Cold.

Probably rain.

And he did it.

He did a previously thought to be impossible thing. Let's read it in Matthew 14.

24 But the ship was now in the midst of the sea, tossed with waves: for the wind was contrary.

25 And in the fourth watch of the night Jesus went unto them, walking on the sea.

26 And when the disciples saw him walking on the sea, they were troubled, saying, It is a spirit; and they cried out for fear.

27 But straightway Jesus spake unto them, saying, Be of good cheer; it is I; be not afraid.

28 And Peter answered him and said, Lord, if it be thou, bid me come unto thee on the water.

29 And he said, Come. And when Peter was come down out of the ship, he walked on the water, to go to Jesus.

I still can't fathom how he did that. But I'm going to learn from it.

The faith required, the trust, the love. It inspires me to get to know Jesus better. Because I think it was in knowing the Master that Peter garnered strength.

He looked to the Lord. He knew him enough to have complete trust. That trust, that faith, that knowing, is what got him out on that water.

If I always had Jesus in my sights, what could I accomplish? If I knew He called to me, if I knew I was on his errand, what would that change?

Confession: I have actually tried to walk on water.

I sank.

Knowing we are on the Lord's errand changes things.

But do we believe He cares about our stuff too? Are we allowed to have our own errands? Or should we always be thinking about Jesus' errands?

Wow, those are deep thoughts. And I don't know if I have all the answers. But here are a couple things I do know.

Of course He cares about our stuff.

We all have "lost items" stories. The endless problems we present that He patiently grants a portion of his power and inspiration in our direction to alleviate. He is so kind to do this for us, so generous. But there is more to it, right?

I know that life is about learning and growing and becoming. And what we are really trying to do is become more like Jesus.

But that involves some trial and error. Maybe more error than trial. But in those attempts, we are doing the best we can with what we have. We are motivated by our desires and also by a guess at what Jesus would like us to do.

And then we try it.

Sometimes we simply do what we want to do. It doesn't seem like something to involve the Lord. Hint: It's always good to involve the Lord.

We try it.

Sometimes our will is aligned with the Lord's. Sometimes not.

We fail or we succeed, and we try again.

I think through this process we learn, and we eventually come to know the Lord, to do what He would do more often. It is a gradual process.

Our desires become His.

We are not becoming a new unrecognizable human. We are becoming our best self which happens when we are aligned with Christ in all things.

Like the prodigal son returning who *came unto himself*, we reveal our *truest* self when we are one with Christ. Our stuff becomes Jesus' stuff, or rather, Jesus' stuff becomes ours.

Let's return to the passage in Matthew of Peter stepping out onto the water.

30 But when he saw the wind boisterous, he was afraid; and beginning to sink, he cried, saying, Lord, save me.

31 And immediately Jesus stretched forth *his* hand, and caught him, and said unto him, O thou of little faith, wherefore didst thou doubt?

32 And when they were come into the ship, the wind ceased.

Peter knew Christ enough to know he could step out onto the water. He knew that when Jesus called, Peter would answer that call. Was his desire to walk on the water like Jesus, aligned with the Lord's will for him? I don't know. But it definitely served to teach a lesson to Peter and to all of us.

The Lord called to him, "Come."

And Peter walked. And he stayed afloat. Somehow the water held his weight.

But then he started to sink.

Jesus was right there in front of him, and Peter started to sink.

As we are reading the account, we are not really aware of the wind or the waves or the storm until Peter is. Could it be that he was not concerned about all the elements at first? He was so focused on the Lord that he was unbothered with any of the other details.

What caused the sinking? His attention wavered. He saw the risks. And he lost sight of the Savior.

Sometimes the first steps are not actually the hardest—that leap into the darkness before the way is illuminated. Peter seemed to handle those just fine.

Sometimes the next steps are more difficult.

The way is lit.

We can actually see the problems.

We see a portion of what we will have to walk through, have to endure, and we don't like it.

We don't see a way out. Our brains think of all the reasons not to do something, and we feel afraid. We second guess.

Distractions come, and we lose our focus on the Lord.

We forget again.

But there is a difficult lesson to learn from Peter.

A path can be thorny and challenging and wrought with trials and still be the correct path.

We are not always immediately rewarded for listening to the Lord in the ways we might be expecting.

Could the waves have increased once Peter left the boat? Did the rain pick up? It might have. Jesus didn't both calm the storm and bid Peter walk on water at the same time.

Peter had to walk through the storm.

I tend to mistakenly use outward examples of prosperity to indicate good choices. *Wow, I made this choice and everything just fell into place.*

But I have had just as many experiences where I had to plug along through hard things wondering why on earth I'd made such a choice. And it was still the correct choice.

It sure helps when I hoped I was acting under the Lord's direction. Because a part of me knows that even if it's difficult now, it will all work out for good at some point.

And that is faith.

I guess it also means knowing the Lord will make good of any thing. The hard, the good, the iffy, the scary, God makes it all good somehow.

Even with challenges, doing the right thing is infinitely easier than trying to forge a path of rebellion.

But that right choice brings with it all of life's typical challenges or sometimes even more difficult ones.

Christ didn't live pain free, nor did He promise a pain free path. In fact, we are asked to bear His cross.

His cross was heavy.

His life difficult.

His friends deserted and betrayed him.

He was hated, mocked and then killed.

He was used for his kindness.

He was distrusted and blamed.

People spoke ill of him.

They lied.

They gossiped.

Religious leaders hated and feared him.

Mobs called for His death.

And yet he kept walking. He kept moving forward in the mission He was called to do.

The thing He volunteered to do, the work, God's work, was the hardest thing anyone has ever had to do, ever.

I was about to say, no one said it would be easy. You've heard that quote about it being worth it. But then this scripture came to mind. "Take my yoke upon you...for my yoke is easy and my burden is light. (Matthew 11:29) The Lord himself said that His yoke, his burdens were easy and light. Obviously not free of trial. But what does come? What makes it easy?

I have never met a single person, ever, who has an easy life.

Somethings to think about:

Following Christ does really bring immediate blessings a lot of the time. It's easier to make right choices than wrong choices. We are promised blessings for keeping the commandments. The Lord delights to honor and bless us. The absolute best and happiest and easiest way to live is by following Christ. Choosing the right is the happy life. I don't know how many other ways I could say it. It's all

true. As challenging as life is, it's better with
Christ.

When my husband and I first started out in our
dating relationship, we heard the promises from
prophets, the commandments to read scriptures
every day with our family.

So we did.

We have.

In our twenty-seven years of marriage, and
throughout our engagement, Dustin and I have
missed very few days of scripture reading or prayer.
And the blessings have been profound, beautiful,
eternal.

We have been filled with joy and power and
love.

Striving to be close to God has been a lifelong
goal for each of us. Our family has figuratively
walked with Christ. We have tried to follow Him.
We count it as our greatest joy and desire.

Blessings come from following our Savior,
temporal and spiritual blessings more wonderful
than we can possibly imagine. The Lord delights in
it. And we see that. We see His blessings. The
feeling in our home is special. Our hearts lean away
from contention. We find that the influence of Satan
is less. We love the blessings that come from
reading the scriptures.

But that still isn't addressing the fact that it's also hard.

Painfully hard.

How is it easy and hard?

When my sweet daughter was born, she was immediately hospitalized at one week with a severe kidney infection. That lead to many tests, most of them invasive and difficult and painful. Her condition was diagnosed and a plan in place. But even still, one week later, she returned to the hospital. The infection had returned. After two full weeks in the hospital with my newborn and two years of prophylactic antibiotic treatment with regular check ins and invasive difficult tests, we went to see the urologist with the hope that we could avoid a surgery involving three major organs in her body.

But despite constant prayers and thirty-six hours of fasting (which I don't recommend. Twenty-four is sufficient), the doctor was insistent that she did indeed need to have the surgery. I was crushed. It felt like such a personal no. Why would God say no? Why require the surgery? Why didn't he just give us this blessing?

I never really learned that answer to that why.

The day for the surgery came. I brought my sweet two-year-old to the hospital and handed her over to the anesthesiologist and watched while they took her away. The moment I had desperately prayed to avoid was upon me.

And it was okay.

It was more than okay.

The doctors and nurses were full of light. I felt certain of heavenly help. I was lifted and carried. I knew the Lord was with me and her. I knew she would be protected. And a piece of heaven sat with me all the while.

The biggest blessing of all. The reason trials can be easier comes from the beautiful sustaining power and peace that comes into our lives and our hearts in the middle of the worst possible situations. We are lifted and carried and strengthened beyond our own abilities to handle piercingly difficult challenges. We feel better even when life is not yet better. We feel strong even when our strength is tested. We feel calm when the world is in pieces and the storm rages.

Peter carried that assurance with him out onto the water. It wavered only when he lost sight of the Lord. And the dangers and discomfort around him became more powerful in his mind.

We must not let concerns and fears in. We cannot let the storm inside.

At times I think it is a matter of letting go. Let's talk for a minute about acceptance.

What if instead of seeing the waves and wind and rain and being afraid, what if Peter looked at it all and thought, *yes, it's raining on me. The waves are crashing onto me. Maybe bigger waves are coming. I'm drenched. I don't like this. But, I'm standing. I'm walking. I'm doing it. There's Jesus. I guess I have to walk with a storm going on. I guess I have to keep going. I guess this is the plan.*

And then he kept walking?

I think maybe part of my problem is the fighting against the trial. I don't like being uncomfortable. I don't want to feel pain. I don't want to lose loved ones. I don't want….any number of things. But if I accept the hardship and stop fighting, if I accept the pain, feel sad, pay attention to where I am, see the Lord in my life. And keep going?

When Peter stopped walking, did he sink to his death? Was his hope gone? Had he failed?

No.

The Lord reached out His hand and lifted him back into his eternal embrace. I wonder how he got back to the boat. Did they walk together? Was Peter carried?

The faith to walk leads us down some treacherous territory sometimes, but never alone and never without all the sustaining help we need.

And when I sink, He lifts me up, and we try again.

I trust the Lord. If I keep Him in my sights, I remember that I trust Him. And that for me, is how the burden is light.

Even when it's terribly painful.

With Christ, it is less so. We see that pain and joy, happiness and sorrow, worry and peace can exist in the same human heart at the same time. With that comes the assurance that even if we sink like Peter, it really is all going to be OK.

3

I TRUST GOD. I'VE SEEN WHAT HE CAN DO

The Earth is amazing. The One who created all of this magnificence, all the community in ecosystems, the glorious beauty, the balance between all the elements is someone I can trust.

He is the same person who helped me know to visit my dad before he died.

He helped me know to visit my Mission President before he died.

He helped me know about simple things like the amount of tables and centerpieces needed for big activities.

He guided me for years in the middle of the night when children were crying and had earaches.

He tells me when to call them, when to say something, when to wait and watch.

He helps me when I try to teach, to love and to serve.

I see His hand bringing me home, showing me how to be better, how to love better, how to repent.

I see the results of listening to Him ... and not listening.

And I know He is the one.

He's the one to trust, to obey, to follow, to be like. He is it.

He is strong.

Have you considered that with the simple words, "I am He," the Roman soldiers who were come to take him, backed up and fell to the ground?

3 Judas then, having received a band *of men* and officers from the chief priests and Pharisees, cometh thither with lanterns and torches and weapons.

4 Jesus therefore, knowing all things that should come upon him, went forth, and said unto them, Whom seek ye?

5 They answered him, Jesus of Nazareth. Jesus saith unto them, I am *he*. And Judas also, which betrayed him, stood with them.

6 As soon then as he had said unto them, I

am *he,* they went backward, and fell to the ground. John 18.

No one and no thing is stronger than our Lord, no group, no country, no temptation, no fear.

He helps with the small things.

I mentioned lost things. How many times has He helped you find your keys?

When I'm desperately looking for something, I eventually pray because I have no other way to remember where the thing might be. But I feel like it is too small a thing, like there are so many more important things I should be praying for. But here I am, asking about the keys again. And He helps. Every time.

The most memorable of times I lost the keys, I was at girls camp. Not having my keys meant I couldn't drive my car home. My husband was contacting people at home to a spare up for me—a five hour drive. I didn't know what to do. And I felt prompted to ask everyone to pray to help find my keys. So they announced it, and they prayed, and about two hundred girls went on a mad search to find them. And within minutes, someone shouted victory.

I immediately prayed with the small group, surrounding one teenage girl, triumphantly holding my car keys, thanking God for helping us. He was too good, too wonderful.

The keys were in a back seat pocket of someone's car.

The girl who found them said she knew she would be the one, and she really listened to the spirit.

Remarkably, the whole camp was affected by this evidence that God cares about us. Many of the girls bore their testimony about it. That experience is a large-scale example of what happens all the time. Heavenly Father does help us with even the smallest cares and wishes.

He knows and cares about each one of us. When you are on his errand, you get a front row seat to His tireless quest to bring His children home.

He really never gives up on us.

A woman who lives near me has stopped attending church. She is lovely and has a wonderful family, but for whatever reason, she had distanced herself from the church congregation.

But she wanted to start writing.

Whose writing group did she join without knowing me at all? Mine, the only person within many miles in the same church congregation as she.

This placed her in a longer term regular friendship with me and opportunities to be cared for and have a good experience with people of faith.

There are no coincidences.

While serving in the Spain Missionary Training Center, my daughter went to a local park to contact people every week. She noticed that they would run into the exact people who would be most blessed that day by a talk with the missionaries. If she had a French speaking companion, they ran into all the French people. Russian speaking? Russians. There was always, every time, evidence that God was trying to reach His children.

He parted the sea so His children could cross and finally be free of slavery.

He calms storms.

He heals.

He guides and loves and comforts and directs. He sits with us in our most painful sorrows as well as our simple defeats. He rises with us in victory. He is there, the King of the universe, the creator of all things, available to us with the simple words of prayer.

He has our best interests in mind. To believe this, you must know Him. You must trust Him, because sometimes He says "No" to our requests.

Praying is not a game where He toys with our

wishes and desires. And He is not Santa Claus, gifting us a list of items.

But rather, He is orchestrating the very best ways and means for us to be happy and return home to Him someday.

If the best decision feels terribly hard in the moment, if we feel lost, ignored or abandoned...

These are difficult things to feel.

But if we are in the middle of a personal storm...

Trust and faith in Him get us through with the hope that good will come.

We have a God on our side who is our Father, who sent His son to suffer and die so that we could have all of the good things possible from living here on the Earth. This God has proven His love and continues to do so every single day.

See that love.

Trust it.

Trust Him.

Have the faith to act.

His plan will be the best path for you.

And He will show you that it is, over and over again.

4

FAITH TO LET GO

To be free of clutter is a beautiful thing.

It takes mental energy to manage clutter. And when it is absent, we feel the peaceful order that ignites action, creativity, power, and peace.

If you have ever moved houses, you know the feeling of staring into a closet with three boxes nearby: to keep, donate, throw away. It is amazing to me how much I have been willing to part with when I'm considering a new start in a new place.

The promise of a simpler, clutter free environment is powerful.

The faith to part with long held items, the memories that fill our minds when we see them again, is a similar faith required to let go of long held habits, old associations that bring us down, practices, traditions, schedules, beliefs, anything that weighs on us. Resentment, bitterness, jealousy, comparison. What else clings to us like the barnacles on a ship? What else eats away at our peace and happiness? Those things are sometimes desperately difficult to cast away. But the work required to lose the things that destroy our happiness is faith.

This faith is the faith to let go.

Sometimes we need to let go of good things.

Too much of a good thing prevents better things from making their way into our lives. In our recent move, while clearing out our house, I had a lot of books. I'm an author. I love books. I collect books. The promise of knowledge and adventure on the cover reels me in like a siren call. But I was never going to read all those books in several lifetimes and I was running out of space for bookshelves. Good things can fill our lives so fully that they hinder progress and block the path of better things coming. And never fear. I did not have to give up all my books. I still have a room full of books and several bookshelves besides. Having the faith to let go clarified my thoughts about which ones were truly valuable to me and which could serve someone else better. Our local library received hundreds of new copies. And I have a fine tuned carefully vetted collection.

Our time can be abused by good things, not allowing the entrance of anything better. How often have you started a show, realizing that it has many episodes, then realizing that the episodes make up many Seasons. A story you began for about forty-five minutes of your time tugs at your curiosity and pretty soon you've spent sixty hours of your life watching it.

There is an endless array of choices and opportunities that fill our time from morning until night, weeks and then months if we let it. If we look at the way we spend our time like the clutter in our homes, it might help us be choosy.

I used to enter the Target spend trap and leave with shopping carts full. Now I raise an eyebrow at one useless thing after another imagining where on earth I would put it. The same thing can be said and done about choices regarding our time, energy, good will, thoughts, happiness. Is such a thing worth the expense and drain on every other part of us?

Sometimes we need to let go of our own harmful behavior.

This could be any number of things. Addictions, habits, poor treatment of others, lust, sin, carelessness, overworking, overzealousness, perfectionism, guilt...

I remember going to sleep many nights as a young mother feeling like I had failed the world. Every moment of imperfection replayed in my mind and I grieved for my children who deserved a perfect mother. I fell asleep to these depressing mantras and woke new every morning ready to try again, only to fail once more.

It took many years for me to understand that if the Lord wanted a perfect mother for my children, he would send kids to grandmas, seasoned women. And even then they would not be perfect, they would simply have more experience. I had to accept my efforts for what they were, imperfect, and trust that whatever I had was enough when partnered with Jesus. He could make up the difference for my sweet children.

In our imperfection, we can improve.

We can repent.

Today just might be the day you decide to walk away from doing that thing that you do that you wish you didn't do, because you know in the end it doesn't make you happy and it's not good for you.

Today is the day to let it go. The faith to let go includes giving up things that are not of God, things that harm us, things that have become a clinging crutch.

But those things do not belong in us. They do not deserve a place in a soul like ours. And with help, we can let them go.

Have the faith to get the help you need to let go of what is harming you.

Have the faith to stop.

Have the faith to repent.

Have the faith to become something better than you are.

Accept growth.

Crave opportunities that challenge you.

Work to be all that you once dreamed you could be.

When we have the faith to let go, it frees us to become.

One time I was carrying the burden of guilt and sin that I didn't quite understand how to lose. I hated feeling the heaviness of disappointing God. I hated thinking I'd done something wrong. And when I prayed, I only felt marginally better. It was as if I knew more work was needed from me to truly be able to let go.

But weeks went by, months, and I continued to

be pestered by a nagging reminder that I was not good enough. And looking back I see that I had already let go of the harmful behavior. What I was clinging too, errantly, was the guilt and feelings of accompanying failure and inadequacy. It was during this time when I had another experience with God helping me have the faith I needed. The faith to receive forgiveness, the faith to let go.

I was reading in the scriptures of a people who wanted to be free of their guilt and sin. They cried out to God to apply the atoning power of Christ in their lives. And when they did, their guilt was swept away replaced by joy. I read that and did the same. I prayed to apply the atonement in my life, allow Jesus' sacrifice that He already made for me to be active and healing, forgive me. I felt a wonderful feeling wash over me. It was tangible and physical as well as emotional and heartfelt. I know God heard me and He was washing me clean. I needed that extra experience to truly believe it would work for me like it worked for others. I needed a bit of help with my faith. At last I was able to let go of the nagging persistent reminder of fault and accept my offerings as imperfect as they are, as a part of my beautiful life.

Yes, we do things wrong. Yes, it is part of our

growth and experience. Yes, we can be forgiven and let it go.

Let go of comparison.

I have a fascination with corners, river bends, and curving paths that move just out of sight.

What is around the bend? I have to know. What's over the next ridge? I must discover it. I must walk there. I have to see.

If I reach a milestone, I look for the next one.

Sometimes I see these milestones in the lives of others.

Gratefully, I have not ever been one to view the accomplishments of others with a scarcity mindset. I am all about abundance. Usually I see someone else's pinnacles as an opportunity waiting for me also to climb. It's proof it can be done.

So I am not plagued with comparison and jealousy in that way.

But I am plagued with a never-ending fascination with "What if" and a curiosity and challenge to see if I too can do the same. In some ways, this abundance mentality is healthy and encourages me to improve. But in other ways it can lead to a sense of dissatisfaction with my current state. Perhaps you are like me. Or perhaps you view others' accomplishments with the deflation of failure, as if the things someone else does have a bearing on your worth or value.

I am so happy that at the end of the day we are not measured against anyone. Our lives are not viewed on a curve. We are simply living and becoming and striving and working to be the best person it is possible for us to become.

No matter if we need to let go of comparison in an abundance or scarcity mindset, comparison might be the very thing we can do without. It might be the thing that truly does rob joy.

My friend used to say look up and not side to side. Go to God for acceptance and validation, for a check-in on how you're doing.

I believe in an oft quoted statement by Walt Whitman, "Happiness not for another time but this time not for another place but this place."

I value my abundance, hope, and excitement about all the possibilities in this marvelous life of ours. I see so much potential for adventure. But I need the faith to love what I have, to accept what is mine and have gratitude for the plentitude around me. I need the faith to let go of the next best thing if it robs the joy of the current life I'm living.

Let go of Relationships.

The faith to let go fits in so many different experiences. Faith to repent. Faith to focus on what matters most, faith to declutter our stuff and our time.

Sometimes we need to let go of the relationships in our lives.

Healthy boundaries, time spent away, cutting off completely, are all things that sometimes require our faith and courage. It can be very difficult to know when and how to distance ourselves from those who might have even been close at one time. But there are absolutely justified and necessary and spirit directed times to run from those who are possibly doing us harm. And in those moments, it can require great faith to let go.

Sometimes those doing us harm have a great hold on our lives.

I had what I thought was a dear friend years ago, but the friendship became toxic to the point of me experiencing the brunt of all her frustrations in a massive rage induced conversation every now and then. I held on way too long, hoping there was something I could do to keep her happy. I allowed the subsequent subtle and more quiet abuse to disturb my peace for too long afterward. Some of the cruelest things I've ever heard or experienced have come at her direction. When at last I had the courage and the fortitude to distance myself and to remain distant, only then did I find peace. Did it feel foreign, anti-Christian or mean to stay away from someone? A bit at times, but the reaffirming closeness to God in prayer and the reassurance that I'd made a good decision helped me trust in that direction and maintain my faith to let go.

My experience is mild compared to some who feel the brunt of cruelty and manipulative control at the hand of family members, spouses, significant others, or at work, church or in their communities.

The faith to let go of these kinds of relationships is perhaps the most difficult to discern and to maintain. I was able to see clearly the trap I was in when I distanced myself for a time. The closer I am to my Savior, the more at peace I feel about my choice to let go.

I can only hope and pray these words will help someone in the toughest of circumstances to have the courage and fortitude to find safe places and people to trust, to lean on our Savior and to begin the process of healing.

Let go of control

I'm an oldest daughter.

The first trip my husband and I took together, I held on to our tickets, boarding passes, passports and driver's licenses. I just felt better knowing I had the important stuff under control.

That was then. I've learned a lot since then. But

it's helpful for me to understand my natural tendencies.

I love a good plan.

But I don't want to be tied down to someone else's spreadsheet.

What can I say?

I'm complicated.

I'm happy to go with the plan as long as I like the plan.

I always prefer if I have a say in the brainstorming of said plan. And I like it the most if I thought of it myself.

Do I sound like a difficult person? I'm really not. At this stage of my life, I've adapted to be way more likable, flexible, and easy going. I often prefer to champion someone else's ideas. And more often than not, I prefer if someone else tells me what to do.

At some point, we give up our quirks. We all do that. We grow, learn, adapt.

If you're like me at all, the biggest thing to let go might be the toughest for some of us but provides the most relief: control.

Can we let go of the control of our lives? Can we give everything to God? Can we rely on His plan, His work, His direction and His counsel and move forward?

Consider the time shortly after the Savior's death.

The Apostles were left on their own to make of things what they would.

They were then in charge of the work.

The entirety of Christ's kingdom in their part of the world rested on their shoulders.

But they were fishing.

And caught nothing.

I have been there. I have tried to continue doing something, wanting it to work, hoping for success, but knowing it was not the time, that I had better things in store and more important things to be doing. I felt like I was forcing success and couldn't find it.

They could not find success in their previous profession. They fished all night and caught nothing.

They didn't seem to realize it, but they had better things to be doing.

The Savior appeared to them, told them where to cast their nets. They caught more fish than they ever had before, boats full.

And then He told them what they really needed to be doing.

Fishing, working out a livelihood probably

made sense to them. They probably needed food. Their families needed support.

But Jesus showed that if he needed fish, he could find fish.

And He has promised to care for His workers in His kingdom. "Consider the lilies of the field," He said.

What He needed were workers in His kingdom.

"Feed my sheep," He said over and over again, three times to Peter.

And the apostles learned to let go.

Have the faith to let go of the things that are not God's. And hold on and work for the things that are.

As a side note, sometimes fishing for fish might be just the thing that is needful. Sometimes God helps us with the things we love to do or need to do, too. He helps us have and work for the things we need. The beauty is working hard to know the difference, to know when to let go of our need to collect and grow and succeed and instead, trust our Savior that doing His work will yield the most eternal and lasting results for us and others and for Him and His work. In a beautiful way, doing the Lord's work first, often grows our work too.

Not everyone is so control minded but for those of us who forget to consult with the Master Planner before embarking on our own detailed blue prints, remember to let go.

Let Him write our story.

Let Him guide us and lead us gently along.

If we can build up our trust and hand all our hopes over to Him, it will be much more and much better than we could have ever designed ourselves.

But what about being anxiously engaged in good causes? What about doing things with the agency we have been given?

Acting. Doing. Walking. Creating. Working. These and all the other action verbs relating to living the Gospel are all what this whole book is about. So I'm not really saying we should stop. I'm just saying, don't forget to involve the one who knows the end from the beginning, the one who has a perfect plan for you and me all ready to go. Involve Him and do the best you can with the rest.

Letting go and all its many opportunities sounds great in theory but the actual nitty gritty act of doing it requires something determined inside. It requires strength. It requires resolve.

This inner resource, the backbone of letting go, is faith.

And this faith will grow over time.

No matter what we have to let go, maybe it's one thing or all the things, the more practice we have doing it, the easier it will be and the greater our faith and the stronger our courage.

Even though letting go might hurt in the middle of ripping off the bandaid, it is always also accompanied by a sense of relief. We are lighter and more free when we let go.

I know in whom I trust. And I can let go when it is for Him.

5

FAITH TO MAKE PEACE

As I stood at the top of that hill in Brazil, enveloped by sudden darkness, I felt the power of Peace.

It was calming, comforting, strengthening.

I wished to always feel that way.

But from our early days in preschool, through emotional teenage years and into adulthood, there seems to always be something going on that disturbs peace.

So admittedly, this is a chapter discussion in which I would love to listen at *your* feet and learn.

It's probably safe to say almost all of us have one person or another in our lives who is at odds with us. The level of contention we might feel as a result probably varies per situation.

It's difficult to even drive on a freeway without feeling animosity from someone.

So for those of us who are highly sensitive to contention and unease, these kinds of interactions steal our peace.

I used to read the Bible verses that talk about going to our brother and trying to fix the contention between us and them and ask my self if there was more I could be doing to help those that don't like me or are angry with me or seem to be at odds with me. Some in my life don't even communicate those things with words. There is just a sense of unexplained distance that reads as contention to me.

I would feel guilt that anyone was annoyed with me. Surely it must be my duty to fix whatever was causing their dislike.

Typing that sounds a bit ridiculous. But it was real to me, and I'm certain there are some of you reading that have felt the same.

Some of us take pride in being liked, in being so likable that we are not at odds with anyone. That kind of person will feel crushed when the inevitable person doesn't like them.

Some of us are sensitive and easily hurt.

Some of us are afraid.

And some of us are easy to ignite, to annoy and to bother.

As time has gone on, I have changed my thoughts about blame and my capacity for internal peace.

Yes, I do think we need to do all we can to encourage unity and peace in our circles.

Depending on the purpose of the relationship in our lives, some relationships deserve more long-suffering and endurance and patience to be able to heal.

But there are plenty of relationships that simply do not need to be weighted in our peaceful standing. We do not need to give them power to affect our happiness. Their disquiet with us could be caused by any number of things in their lives and inside them that we could not affect no matter how perfectly we behaved.

And some relationships are simply not safe for us.

The man flipping us off on the freeway, for example, does not deserve space in our thoughts, nor does he deserve a chance to disrupt our peace.

And we should run from our abusers.

Sometimes we have done what is possible for a relationship and still someone might continue to withhold forgiveness or simply not wish to be around us.

I'm learning how to feel at peace with my own

efforts and how to feel at peace with the *Lord* even if others might be at odds with me.

All efforts to arrive at whatever peace is possible require great faith whether we need the faith to walk away and let something be, to give something space, or to work harder and longer to make something heal.

The faith walk for peace involves inner work and external work.

And there is a great need in the world for those who are working to bring about peace—for the peacemakers.

Power from the Author of Peace is available for the maker of peace wherever he or she might be. Jesus is the expert, and He wants us all at peace. He will help us.

The only way I can imagine any of us surviving this world of contention is by accessing God's power and understanding and discernment.

Great blessings result especially as we remember that every person here is greatly loved by our Maker.

"Blessed are the peacemakers for they shall be called the children of God." (Matthew 5:9)

If we can make peace with each other, love each other, give space for each other, we are acting as a family. We are God's children. We are siblings and will be called the children of God.

There are some people gifted at making peace. They know just what to say. They bring out reconciliation in contentious relationships or even just use humor in perfect ways that ease tense feelings.

But not everyone has this gift. Some of us awkwardly stumble over words or run away from contention without resolving it.

Whether we are blessed with a natural gift or are simply learning how to improve, we all can become practiced at it, at building bridges, at making it easy to be at ease with a person, and helping others feel peace.

Are your actions and your words raising the drama of a situation or diffusing it? Do you spread gossip and revel in the stories of other people's lives? Or do you smooth things over, communicate carefully and positively and de-escalate when possible?

Are you someone who wants your friends to hate your enemies? Do you have enemies? Sometimes tactics learned in middle school and on reality TV are prevalent in real life adult relationships. Even if everyone around us behaves in this kind of culture, one person can change the feeling of a group, one person can bring light, love, patience and Christlike reactions to others. I've seen one person change the atmosphere and vibe of hundreds.

Great faith is required to be that one. To bury hurt and forgive, to give place for people to start anew, to forgive. All the things that are needed in peacemaking require our faith.

Every day there are ways to help heal our world, and they might seem small, but by now we all know that there are no small things, really. Small things bring about what is great, over and over again.

In a world filled with misunderstanding, division, and conflict, the ability to bring peace is a gift —one that requires faith, and, most importantly, a willingness to reach out to others with compassion.

Becoming an effective peacemaker doesn't mean avoiding conflict or remaining passive. Inner unspoken antagonism is still contention.

It does call for dedication. It calls for a commitment to finding resolution, bridging divides, and helping others walk toward understanding and reconciliation. It calls for Faith.

Relationships take work.

Every bit of effort we put toward peace with others is an act of Faith. God wants us to act as brothers and sisters that we may be His children.

He tenderly, carefully watches over us.

What makes God sad? What would ever make Him cry?

In Moses we learn that we can make Him cry. Our mistreatment of one another causes God great sorrow. "How canst thou weep?…They are without affection and hate their own blood." (Moses 7)

And our ability to at last be united together in one brings Him great joy, so much so that He brought an entire city up into Heaven with Him when they accomplished such a Zion like peaceful state. (Moses 7)

Peace within and with our fellow brothers and sisters on this Earth may at times seem impossible.

A brief study on some peacemaking tips can help.

The following list might offer a starting point of practical ways to implement peacemaking.

1. Developing Empathy: Seeing Through Another's Eyes

TO TRULY UNDERSTAND someone else's perspective, we must be willing to step outside our own thoughts and emotions and see the world through their eyes. This shift requires humility and an openness to experiences that differ from our own.

We need to look in the mirror and say,

"You beautiful human, you do not know everything. You have so much to learn."

Admit that and take it to heart and then begin a lifelong effort to learn from other people.

Really seeing someone else and feeling what they feel helps.

One time my son was going to be closely associating with a man who I disagreed with on most things. I had some misgivings about allowing him to spend so much time with my son, even though I was present for all of it. I viewed him more as a threat than another human, until one day he was walking away and while watching the back of him on a foggy night, I was filled with a sense of his loneliness. And I understood him in a way I never had before. I knew those feelings were a gift from God. I was gifted a tiny bit of empathy.

And I was grateful.

We are now dear friends.

I do think empathy can be practiced and learned. If we pay close attention to others and our own levels of empathy, we can become better.

Ways to practice empathy include:

-Listen without interrupting: Give the other person the space to speak fully before responding. Active listening shows respect and fosters connection.

-Ask open-ended questions: Try to understand not just what someone is saying but why they feel the way they do.

-Acknowledge their emotions: Recognize and validate their feelings, even if you don't agree with their conclusions.

It is likely that two people with differing views can both be right. We view the world around us from a unique perspective.

Empathy helps dissolve barriers that cause conflicts to fester. When people feel understood, they are often more open to finding common ground and reaching peaceful resolutions.

2. Communication as a Tool for Peace

CLEAR, respectful communication is a vital skill for peacemakers. Too often, conflict arises from misunderstandings or poor communication. By practicing active listening, choosing our words carefully, and maintaining a respectful tone, we can avoid many potential conflicts and defuse existing ones.

Effective communication as a peacemaker involves:

-Avoiding blame: Speak from your perspective using "I" statements, which reduce defensiveness and promote openness. For example, "I feel upset when…" instead of "You always make me…"

-Being direct but kind: Don't evade difficult topics. Speak honestly but with sensitivity. Ignoring difficult topics sometimes just breeds inner contention which is not peaceful.

-Clarifying misunderstandings: If something isn't clear, ask questions instead of making assumptions.

When we communicate effectively, we foster an atmosphere of respect and openness, creating fertile ground for peace to take root and grow.

3. Embracing Patience

PEACEMAKING IS OFTEN A SLOW PROCESS, requiring patience, tolerance, and a willingness to let go of the need for immediate resolution. There will be times when peace feels impossible, when emotions run high, and when the gap between perspectives seems insurmountable. That's okay. It takes time. Sometimes the most peaceful path is space between parties. But peace is still possible.

To cultivate patience:

-Accept imperfection: Not every conflict will resolve perfectly. Sometimes, peace means agreeing to disagree.

-Give others space to process: Some people need time to consider another perspective or to let emotions settle.

-Focus on small steps: Sometimes, peace is built one small step at a time. Acknowledge and celebrate progress, however minor.

4. Practicing Forgiveness: Letting Go of Resentment

We may not want to admit it, but true peace cannot coexist with grudges or resentment. And perhaps, even if someone in our life is at odds with us, we do not need to be at odds with them. When we forgive, we release the hold of past hurts and open up to healing and reconciliation.

To cultivate forgiveness:

-Recognize forgiveness as a choice: It is not about forgetting or condoning wrong actions but about releasing their hold on your heart.

-Empathize with the offender: Try to see things from their perspective, as this can help you understand why they acted as they did. I acknowledge that abusive situations need to be handled differently. Empathy and accepting abuse are two different things.

-Commit to moving forward: Shift your focus from the past to the future, envisioning a path forward free from bitterness. And if necessary, free from the person doing you harm.

What if we were able to view every person as though they were beginning from a fresh starting point, that moment, that day. Could we begin again with everyone we know? I do believe that is how the Savior sees us, as a clean fresh slate of potential.

Forgiveness frees us to build new, more peaceful relationships, allowing both sides to move beyond the conflict and into mutual understanding. Or it simply allows us to let go of conflict in our hearts and feel inner peace as well as the freedom to no longer contend with an antagonizer.

5. Encouraging Collaborative Problem-Solving

Peacemaking is not about solving all problems alone. Rather, it involves encouraging collaboration and inviting others to participate in finding solutions. When people work together, they become invested in the outcome, which makes lasting peace more achievable.

I've been doing more interfaith work lately and their examples in mutual understanding and collaboration are empowering to me. Recently I witnessed panel discussions between a Muslim Imam and Jewish Rabbi. They acted as brothers with mutual respect and desire to collaborate even while each felt differences of opinion about the other that will not be resolved any time soon.

Ways to foster collaboration:

-Focus on shared goals: Identify common interests and build on them. For example, both parties might want stability, respect, or a harmonious environment.

-Encourage brainstorming: Invite everyone involved to propose solutions and ideas, creating a sense of collective ownership.

-Facilitate compromise: Help each side make

concessions for the greater good. Emphasize the importance of meeting halfway.

Collaboration transforms a confrontational approach into a cooperative one, making it easier to build sustainable peace.

6. Leading by Example: Being the Change You Want to See

As PEACEMAKERS, our actions speak louder than words. Living by the principles we espouse is one of the most powerful ways to inspire peace in others. When people see us acting with kindness, patience, and integrity, they are more likely to follow suit.

To lead by example:

-Be consistent: Let your behavior reflect the values you promote, even in challenging situations.

-Show kindness and compassion: Offer a gentle response, even when others are hostile.

-Model conflict resolution: Demonstrate constructive ways to handle disagreements, showing others that peaceful outcomes are possible.

By embodying the qualities of a peacemaker, we become more practiced and expert at the methods and we can model hope and possibility for others.

Walking in the Way of Peace

Becoming an effective peacemaker is not a one-time achievement but a lifelong journey. Each day brings new opportunities to practice patience, empathy, and understanding, to listen and to communicate with respect. Every effort we make toward peace is an act of Faith and would also bring us closer to the great peacemaker, Jesus Christ Himself.

It requires discernment to know what is the best step to take when contention affects us. Walking away and putting in work both require faith and careful understanding.

Peacemaking is work at the very edges of faith, sometimes stepping into the darkness of the unknown with compassion, knowing that peace is worth the effort, that it is a gift we can offer ourselves and the world. And as we walk this path, we help others find their way toward peace, illuminating the way to healing, understanding, and unity.

6

THE INTERFAITH WALK

I've been doing a lot of listening lately.

And attending meetings and doing service and working side by side with people not of my faith.

I've spent my entire life mostly surrounded by people in multiple religions and with varying beliefs.

I enjoy the difference and the diversity and the creativity of a group of different but like minded people.

But lately I've been doing more listening and collaborating and really seeking to learn from others in a much more sharply focused way.

And I've come to appreciate even more that I'm

surrounded by some remarkable faithful people in my particular religion and outside of it.

One time I sat on a board of a local community theater, and I had the opportunity write a play they would then produce.

It was a huge endeavor by all of us to write, direct and produce this play. On the day of its first performance, we were working hard and detail after detail became more difficult as one thing after another fell through.

A fellow woman on the board stopped me in the rush in the middle of a crowded theater foyer, grabbed my hands and said, "Let us pray."

She then proceeded to huddle close and say the words out loud that had been in my heart for weeks. "Lord, bless our efforts," followed by many more pleadings, asking specifically for all the various things we needed. And then she began in a tender way to praise God and thank Him. It was beautiful.

I felt a bit chastened that I had not thought to pray with our group that day, nor had I ever considered stopping in the middle of a crowded foyer to pray with another person out loud.

It reminded me of the time I had served with a group, supporting and loving survivors of domestic violence. We fed the ladies lunch once a month and provided fun services like pedicures and manicures and gifts of time and mentoring.

At the end of every event, the leader of the group would invite women to come forward to a line of us, standing ready at the side of the room. These women approached one by one, and we would take their hands and pray for them, in that moment, right then, pleading for God to send down His love and power and protection in their behalf.

I was so touched to participate as someone saying the prayers for woman after woman, their hands clutching mine, their heads bowed, their soft whispers of Amen, fueling my faith and desire to help them.

I know God heard those prayers.

He hears all of them. He hears the prayers of people of other faiths, who speak different languages, who are living on opposite sides of the world.

He hears the prayers of our enemies. He hears and loves those who do us harm.

We are all His children.

One time I sat in a meeting listening to the producer of a well known depiction of the Savior and His life.

He said something like "We are bringing people to Jesus. We can let Him take care of the rest."

I loved that.

And I extended that notion to mean something even more broad than bringing people to Jesus.

I believe in strengthening people's faith, wherever it may lie, trusting that God can do miracles with even the tiniest bit of faith.

If someone needs a course correction, He will help them. Our job is to love and invite and to support and strengthen faith.

So many different religions and faith practices are doing so much good in the lives of others. Why stand in their way? Why argue points of doctrine?

Everyone keep doing the good that you're doing.

If someone thinks about God differently than I do, that's OK, strengthen their faith in God.

Should we be afraid of another's faith?

No.

What about scriptures that counsel not to let unworthy people be our teachers?

That scripture is misquoted and misrepresented all the time.

We can learn from people who are different than we are.

Now and then we see evidence of an extreme-type faith group having an evil influence on their followers. Let's not let those examples ruin our trust in the faith of others. If it is doing good, the fruits of their faith are good, then we should be building and strengthening their efforts. I stand by this.

We can learn from the differences between us all.

And we should.

The biggest ugliest most deadly wars are caused and fueled by people who cannot come to agreement about religion. Every single mass genocide, every ethnic cleansing, had religious differences at the heart.

People are not changed by politics.

People are changed by their different religions.

If we as a faithful and religious people cannot lead out in love and collaboration and listening and growing together in an interfaith way, or at least support those who are doing so, we will never be able to heal the problems in our world.

Or in our neighborhoods, our cities, our homes.

In our own personal lives.

In our hearts.

It all starts with listening and supporting and loving.

Right now. In our own circles.

Are you close friends with someone who believes differently than you do?

I love the word, collaborate.

Hand in hand, we can do much more than each of us separately trying to do good.

I was recently involved with the communication and publicizing of a live Nativity and Bethlehem experience in our town.

It was the perfect blend of cooperation between city, charities, and another church who jointly sponsors the event with ours.

Everyone worked hard together to produce something truly beautiful. Eight thousand people came to see the results of their efforts.

The Mayor spoke at the event, declaring the city better and blessed for our presence in it.

It was a beautiful weekend and came about as successful as it was, in part because of the collaboration we did with those outside our faith.

Amazing.

Our school offers a service associated with high school graduation called Baccalaureate.

It has historically been held at a local Methodist church. Their sanctuary is beautiful. The community comes together to hear many faith leaders share positive messages with the graduates and their families.

In recent years a beautiful shift in the programming has blessed our town. The volunteer moms in charge asked the student body to sign up if they wished to participate in the event by sharing their faith.

Many signed up. These beautiful students sang and prayed and shared scriptures and inspirations.

A group of choir students of all different faiths sang together.

We ended the evening having heard from the Muslim, Baha'i, Hindu, Jewish, and Christian faiths of many denominations.

I always leave so proud of our students and their desires to share their faith with others.

I leave having hope for our community. Every time.

If we can support and participate in an assembly of people sharing all different kinds of faith, we can do so on smaller scales in our lives and in our circles…and on larger scales across towns, blending borders and building bridges between communities.

This is my hope, to have one community with all the varying and beautiful beliefs working together.

And it starts with the one, with me.

I'd love for you to join me.

7

FAITH TO CREATE

I've been digging in the dirt lately.

And walking for hours on trails in the woods.

And floating out on the water in the middle of a lake.

And hiking up mountains.

And listening to birds sing.

And planting milkweed for the Monarchs.

I've been outside as much as I possibly can be.

And being with God's creations has healed places inside me I didn't know were unwell.

He really is the Great Creator.

I love to see the beauty all around us on Earth. It has form and function and that would be enough. But then on top of a useful place, it is beautiful.

And not just beautiful. It steals my breath, brings tears to my eyes, and fills my soul. And it was designed to do so. By the Great Creator.

I am in awe of the processes and the connections between all living things. Water gives off ions that bring peace and a sense of well being. The sounds of birds, rain, falling water all bring peace. Specific aromas of dirt, flowers, grass, trees, water, all work to heal us. Some smells and sounds are meant to be a warning. Others are there to energize and uplift. Some to put us to sleep.

It's incredible that in my yard I have flowers that only bloom at night, and they're glorious and smell amazing. I went out to see them the other evening and was surprised by a large black and white moth. There is an actual moth whose purpose it is to pollinate night blooming flowers.

So many miracles surround us: Hummingbirds, bees, monarchs and their journey, their necessities provided for by the Milkweed plant. Bioluminescence, moon bows near waterfalls, the changing shells of a hermit crab, the cycle of water…Incredible processes here on earth and all thought up by the greatest most ingenious creator of all time.

And more and more and more.

I could never think up or list all the goodness of God and His creations.

And with all His greatness and immense power and reach and purpose, His eye is upon us. Our bodies in all their wonder are His glorious creations.

And more.

We are His why. (Moses 1:39)

We are why the amazing Earth was created.

We are *children* of the Master Creator.

That means a portion of His great creativity is in us.

Have you thought about that before?

One of our godlike inherited qualities is the desire and ability to create.

The closer we are to God, the more and better we can create. Consider the words of Dieter F. Uchtdorf.

The more you trust and rely upon the Spirit, the greater your capacity to create. That is your opportunity in this life and your destiny in the life to come. Sisters, trust and rely on the Spirit. As you take the normal opportunities of your daily life and create something of beauty and helpfulness, you improve not only the world around you but also the world within you. (https://www.churchofjesuschrist.org/study/

general-conference/2008/10/happiness-your-
heritage?lang=eng)

To create is to introduce something on Earth
that wasn't there before. And it comes in all forms.

Are you creative?

I used to think creative and crafty were the
same thing. If I was creative, I was good with art. I
could paint, sew and make crafts.

While creativity involves those kinds of things,
I think it encompasses far more.

Are you a creative thinker? Do you push boundaries of thought and think outside the box?

Or perhaps you are good with words. Do you
write music? Do you schedule well? Do you run
committees and plan?

Are you the one who can think up imaginary
games for the kids? Do you tell good jokes? Are
you witty? Are you a creator of peace? Do you
create safe places for others?

Creativity is so much more than I have ever
thought.

If we claim no access to this God-given trait
perhaps we don't see the moments we truly create.
Or perhaps we are not nurturing the parts of us that
emulate God in those ways.

Think of all the processes, the thoughts, the

planning, the knowledge that was required in the creation of such a magnificent and complex planet. The laws, the science, the math, the poetry, the compassion and on and on. All have place for creativity.

A much beloved quote by Thomas S. Monson helps us see.

"God left the world unfinished for man to work his skill upon. He left the electricity in the cloud, the oil in the earth. He left the rivers unbridged and the forests unfelled and the cities unbuilt. God gives to man the challenge of raw materials, not the ease of finished things. He leaves the pictures unpainted and the music unsung and the problems unsolved, that man might know the joys and glories of creation." (In Quest of the Abundant Life. March 1988.) https://www.chur chofjesuschrist.org/study/ensign/1988/03/in-quest-of-the-abundant-life?lang=eng

When we nurture our creativity, we're honoring a gift from God, and we're participating in a process that connects us more deeply to Him. This creativity doesn't have to be grand or even visible to others. It could be the way we bring love and beauty to those closest to us, the way we pursue a passion or project with faith and enthusiasm, or even the way we work through our trials, finding growth and transformation.

If you're not sure where to start, look at the things that bring you joy and make you feel alive. Is it cooking a meal for someone you love? Is it solving a tricky problem at work or coming up with a plan that no one else thought of? Or maybe it's caring for a garden, nurturing life from a tiny seed to a full-grown bloom. Whatever it is, that's where your creative spirit lies, and that's where you can feel closest to God as you co-create with Him.

Remember, creativity is not about perfection or productivity. It's about exploration, about letting that spark within you flourish and grow. It's about finding the courage, the faith, to step into something new, trusting that the Creator who gave you this gift will guide you in using it.

That is faith. The faith to create.

When we create, we echo the divine process of creation itself, and we become instruments in God's hands, adding beauty, love, and hope to the world around us.

Perhaps we can do it a little bit more, a little bit better. Perhaps we can think of what we want to leave here for others when we are gone, or what we wish to contribute now while we are here.

The faith to create is a powerful spurring to action. Through it, every true improvement on earth has come to be.

Our very best creations come about when we involve God. You can imagine why. What a gift to be able to tap into that power, into our divine gift.

When I think of the great Creator being born to Earth, to live and walk and experience His own creation, I think about my relationship with Him and with His work. I think of his hands brushing along the petals of flowers. I consider the trees and the water and his feet on the sand. Did the earth wish to rise up to meet Him where he stood?

And then I think about how much I love my creations.

Writing books requires great strength and a large dose of Faith. Every project is made, pushing through negativity, self doubt and fatigue. Every project contains moments in its creation where I don't know what comes next. I don't know how to make it worthy. Faith carries me through. I know that I am using a God given gift. I know I can try to make good with it. And the rewards are great.

Even though faith is required to push through or to even begin, the joy in creation is still real. All my writing brings me joy. I write books. I create stories, essays, posts, poems, and nonfiction. In a very real way, these are my creations, my contributions to the world. I find it difficult to describe the feelings of satisfaction and accomplishment that fill me whenever I complete another project. Even if no one were to ever read it, I am filled with joy when I create.

To think I have left things on this earth that weren't here before that will be here now because of me, I am kind of in awe of the idea.

But the first time I did so, the very first book that was published for others to read, scared me. I couldn't sleep the night before I knew the book was going live on Amazon. My hands shook as reviews started to come in. I sent that baby out into the world with all the faith I could muster, faith that something in me, something that translated to those pages, was needed in the world.

Faith is required to create.

Faith is required to *share* our creations.

We are meant to do so. We came here to be ourselves, to add our contributions to those that have come before. We are meant to leave the place with a piece of ourselves, changed because we are here.

So often we can't see it. We don't see how our mark on the earth could possibly be left.

I'm seeing in my mind a beautiful soul plugging

along in life with everything fraying at the edges. She's trying to keep her head up but it is very heavy. She is busy living for others. And she doesn't think she is leaving her mark on the world. I see you. I see how creativity might seem like a foreign entity.

Creativity might feel like a luxury you will never have.

You being YOU is often the best thing you can do for our world. That's it. Keep being you.

And be open to the possibility that God wants you to create and He will help you.

Consider the spark of joy you might feel in creation.

All you need is your brain. Creativity isn't about forcing something out of you. It's about letting yourself be YOURSELF. Give yourself the gift of some mind-wandering to joyful things. Creativity will come.

Nurture the creativity in you. Find the manner in which you are the most you. In that place, you will find the buds of creativity beginning to bloom.

While we are busy budding our own creative efforts, we can support others' creative attempts.

Sometimes the new thing, the bold thing, the different and creative thing receives the most suppression.

Resist that inclination.

Welcome the new, the bold, the different.

As we work to become and to create and to contribute, we are emulating our Savior and fulfilling one of the many reasons we were sent to Earth.

In doing so, we have joy and satisfaction and find purpose.

In doing so, we become who we were meant to be.

In doing so, we are a tiny bit more like the Great Creator who gave us this gift.

8

FAITH TO BE YOU

I AM.

Jesus introduces himself as I AM.

"I am that I am." (Exodus 3:14-15)

"Before Abraham was, I am." (John 8:56-59)

"Listen to the voice of Jesus Christ, The great I am." (D&C 29:1)

I certainly don't pretend to understand all the meanings of those two words or the names of Christ, nor do I understand Hebrew.

But I AM sounds permanent. It is a state of being. And it defines a person. Usually we follow the words I AM with something, a modifier or a descriptor. I am tired. I am sad. I am beautiful.

But what does it mean to simply be? If I AM is the full phrase, does that simply mean, Jesus Christ is. He always is. He is HIM, himself, the Savior, now yesterday and tomorrow. He will forever be.

He has said he is the same yesterday today and forever.

And there is something wonderfully comforting about that.

It would also mean that Jesus is always the same Jesus in all situations. He is not one way with one group and then another way with another group. He is always Jesus. He is.

And He wouldn't try to be different depending on what he hoped to gain. If he is the same, then he is the same.

I AM.

What if we were always the same? Not that we stopped growing, learning or becoming, but what if our integrity was so real, our image so authentic, our words, thoughts and actions all true and real all the time?

We didn't change or adjust depending on who we were with. We told the same story to all the people. There were no other versions saved for one group or another. We put forth the same effort no matter who we were with. We showed the same love.

I think this would take a lot of faith, like the faith to walk. This faith is the faith TO BE.

Do we trust that our authentic self is the best thing to offer another? Or are we worried that if people knew what was really inside, we would not be as successful? Do we cater our offering of self based on what we hope to gain?

The story of the Prodigal Son is so touching and instructive. There are many beautiful moments: The father watching for his son, the welcoming embrace, the returning home, the fatted calf, the realization for the oldest that he always had the calf. He always had the sacrifice available and had he yet utilized it? There are many things to learn from the beautiful parable. But one of the most hopeful and empowering moments for me is the phrase, "He came to himself."

He came to himself.

The prodigal son was eating the food of the pigs. He had nothing left and nowhere else to go, and he came to himself.

He remembered who he was.

He started thinking like his real self.

And then he acted.

The prodigal son's misdirection and sins and separation did not define him. Just like our sins and weaknesses do not define us. His truest best repentant self was the man who woke up and returned home, the person who made the best choices.

We too find our very best selves in our truest form.

The best person we can be is our truest self.

And when we have arrived at the absolute best we can be, it will be like our Savior.

But in our own unique way.

No one else can be who we are.

We fill a space in the universe that is uniquely shaped just like us and no one else can fill that role.

Every time we forget to be ourselves, a very important person is missing from the world.

Repenting and becoming and changing and growing are all about accessing that core of a soul inside that makes up our true self.

It is the person most like our Savior.

It is the one longing for home, to return to our Heavenly Father.

Every other misdirection or deviation is being less than we are, shifting away from our true self.

Have faith to be you.

Trust that it's your best self.

Remember that you can grow and improve by accessing your most authentic self.

And as we focus in on the Savior and His love and light, we become brighter and brighter ourselves.

He is the light we hold up and it fills our life until it is a perfect day.

I AM will always be.

The closer we come to Him, the more we too can become.

Have the faith to let go of all pretense, falseness and disingenuous thought and behavior. You will fit right in where you are meant to be with those you are meant to help. There will be a perfectly shaped YOU hole that you will fill. And everything will seem just a little bit brighter and better in the world.

Thank you for being you.

9

A LEGACY OF FAITH—
EXAMPLES FROM THE BIBLE

Throughout the Bible, we see individuals whose lives were transformed by faith. These stories are more than ancient tales; they are powerful accounts of people who, despite hardships and uncertainties, chose to trust God. Their lives offer a blueprint for how we can exercise faith today.

1. Abraham – Faith to Sacrifice

Abraham, often called the "father of faith," lived a life filled with difficult decisions that tested his trust in God. One of the most powerful demonstrations of Abraham's faith is found in Genesis 22, when God commands him to sacrifice his beloved son, Isaac. Abraham had waited years for the promise of a son and a lineage, and now he was asked to give it all up. Although he didn't understand why God would ask such a thing, Abraham's faith allowed him to obey.

In Genesis 22:8, when Isaac questions him about the sacrificial lamb, Abraham replies, "God himself will provide the lamb for the burnt offering, my son." His unwavering faith in God's provision carried him through this heart-wrenching test. And God did provide, sending an angel to stop him and offering a ram in place of Isaac. Abraham's faith teaches us the power of obedience and trust, even when we cannot see the end. His story reminds us that God honors and rewards faith, even when we are asked to make difficult sacrifices.

2. Moses – Faith to Lead

Moses's life was a journey of faith, from his miraculous survival as an infant to his role as the deliverer of Israel. One of the most remarkable acts of faith in Moses's life occurred when he led the Israelites out of Egypt. Despite his initial hesitation and feelings of inadequacy, Moses trusted God's promise to deliver his people.

As Pharaoh's armies pursued the Israelites to

the Red Sea, Moses demonstrated unwavering faith. In Exodus 14:13, he told the people, "Do not be afraid. Stand firm and you will see the deliverance the Lord will bring you today." When he lifted his staff, God parted the sea, allowing the Israelites to cross on dry ground and then closing it upon their enemies. Moses's faith was not rooted in his own strength or ability but in his complete reliance on God's power. His story teaches us that, even when we feel inadequate, God can work miracles through our faith and willingness to obey.

3. Ruth – Faith to Stay and Trust

The story of Ruth is a beautiful example of faith that manifests as loyalty and trust. After her husband's death, Ruth, a Moabite, was free to return to her people. Instead, she chose to stay with her Israelite mother-in-law, Naomi, declaring, "Where you go I will go, and where you stay I will stay. Your people will be my people and your God my God" (Ruth 1:16). Ruth's faith was courageous; she trusted in God and committed herself to an uncertain future in a foreign land.

Ruth's faith led her to Boaz, a kinsman-redeemer who would eventually become her husband and provide for her and Naomi. Her story shows that faith often means staying when it's easier to leave, trusting in God's provision even when we don't know what the future holds. Ruth's life encourages us to have faith in God's care and to trust that He is working in ways we may not yet see.

4. David – Faith to Face Giants

David's story is one of remarkable courage and faith. As a young shepherd, he faced the giant Goliath when no one else in Israel's army dared. Armed with only a sling, stones, and faith in God, David declared to Goliath in 1 Samuel 17:45, "You come against me with sword and spear and javelin, but I come against you in the name of the Lord Almighty." His faith was not in his own strength but in God's ability to deliver him.

David's victory over Goliath was a triumph of faith, showing that no matter how formidable the obstacle, trust in God can overcome any "giant" in our lives. David's courage reminds us that we do not face our challenges alone; God is with us, and with faith in Him, we can face even the most intimidating trials.

5. Esther – Faith to Act with Courage

Esther's story is a testament to the power of faith and courage in the face of danger. As queen of Persia, Esther learned that a decree had been issued to annihilate the Jewish people. She was faced with a choice: remain silent and preserve her position, or risk her life by approaching the king uninvited to plead for her people.

In Esther 4:16, she famously declares, "If I perish, I perish." Esther's faith gave her the strength to act, even at the risk of her own life. She trusted that God had placed her in this position for a reason, and through her bravery, the Jews were saved from destruction. Esther's faith encourages us to act courageously, even when the stakes are high, trusting that God has placed us where we are for a purpose.

6. Daniel – Faith in the Lion's Den

Daniel's faith was unshakable, even in the face of death. When a decree was issued forbidding prayer to anyone except the king, Daniel continued his practice of praying openly to God. His loyalty to God led to him being thrown into a den of lions, but Daniel's faith remained firm.

In Daniel 6:22, after being miraculously saved, Daniel says, "My God sent his angel, and he shut the mouths of the lions." Daniel's faith was rooted in his absolute trust in God's protection. His courage reminds us that faith sometimes requires us to stand alone, even against powerful opposition, and trust that God will sustain us in the face of fearsome trials.

7. Paul – Faith to Persevere Through Trials

The Apostle Paul's life is one of tireless faith, perseverance, and devotion. Once a persecutor of Christians, Paul experienced a powerful conversion on the road to Damascus. From that moment, he dedicated his life to preaching the gospel, enduring shipwrecks, beatings, imprisonment, and constant threats to his life.

In 2 Corinthians 12:9-10, Paul recounts that he pleaded with the Lord to remove a particular "thorn in the flesh," but the Lord responded, "My grace is sufficient for thee: for my strength is made perfect in weakness." Paul accepted this answer, responding with faith: "Therefore I will boast all the more gladly about my weaknesses, so that Christ's power may rest on me."

Paul's faith enabled him to endure unimaginable hardships, trusting that God's grace would sustain him. His life reminds us that faith doesn't always mean a life free from suffering; rather, it means that God's power will sustain us through our trials.

8. Mary – Faith to Accept God's Will

Mary, the mother of Jesus, displayed profound faith when she accepted the role given to her by God. When the angel Gabriel appeared to her and announced that she would bear the Son of God, her response was one of humility and trust: "Behold the handmaid of the Lord; be it unto me according to thy word" (Luke 1:38).

Mary's faith allowed her to accept an unimaginable responsibility with grace and strength. Her story reminds us that faith sometimes requires us to accept God's will, even when it takes us down a path we never expected. Like Mary, we are invited to trust that God's plans are greater than our own, even when we don't fully understand them.

Conclusion: Faith that Endures

Each of these biblical figures shows us a different dimension of faith. Abraham had the faith to sacrifice, Moses had the faith to lead, Ruth had the faith to stay, David had the faith to face giants, Esther had the faith to act with courage, Daniel had the faith to stand firm, Peter had the faith to step forward, Paul had the faith to persevere, and Mary had the faith to accept. Their stories remind us that faith is multifaceted, sometimes requiring sacrifice, other times courage, endurance, or humility.

The lives of these men and women are legacies of faith, written to inspire us to trust God no matter our circumstances. We may not face lions or giants, but our daily challenges still call for the same enduring faith. Through these examples, we are invited to live with the same trust and courage, knowing that the same God who strengthened them is present with us, ready to guide us through every step of our journey.

10

FAITHFUL WITNESSES— EXAMPLES OF FAITH IN THE BOOK OF MORMON

F aith, as we find it in the scriptures, is both a simple belief and an active trust. It's the confidence in unseen promises, the assurance that God will make good on His word. In the lives of ancient prophets and writers, faith wasn't just a quiet hope—it was a dynamic force that shaped their lives, propelled them forward in times of trial, and inspired generations to follow.

1. Nephi – Faith to Move Forward in
    the Dark

One of the earliest stories of profound faith in the Book of Mormon is Nephi's journey with his family into the wilderness. When the Lord commanded Lehi and his family to leave Jerusalem, they had little information about their destination and no clear roadmap. It was a test of obedience and trust, and in the face of overwhelming uncertainty, Nephi's faith remained steady.

In 1 Nephi 3:7, Nephi famously states, "I will go and do the things which the Lord hath commanded, for I know that the Lord giveth no commandments unto the children of men, save he shall prepare a way for them that they may accomplish the thing which he commandeth them." This declaration wasn't a one-time proclamation—it became a theme in Nephi's life. He knew that, although he couldn't see the way, God would make one.

His faith carried him through countless trials: leaving Jerusalem, retrieving the brass plates, and journeying across the wilderness and the ocean. Even when faced with adversity from his own family, Nephi showed resilience, relying on his faith to carry him forward. This faith in God's promises became a guiding principle for him and serves as a powerful reminder for us today. Like Nephi, we can step into the unknown with confidence, knowing that when God commands, He also provides.

2. Alma the Elder – Faith to Trust in God's Deliverance

Alma the Elder's conversion and his subsequent journey of faith began when he heard the prophet Abinadi's courageous testimony before King Noah. Inspired by Abinadi's words, Alma recognized the truth and repented, eventually fleeing to teach and baptize others in secret. Alma's faith in Abinadi's message marked a turning point in his life, and he went on to become a leader for many in the land of Helam.

Later, when Alma and his people were oppressed by the Lamanites, Alma turned to God with unwavering trust. In Mosiah 24, we read that they were forbidden to pray out loud, yet they continued to pour out their hearts in silent prayer. In verses 13–14, the Lord comforts them, saying, "Lift up your heads and be of good comfort, for I know of the covenant which ye have made unto me... I will also ease the burdens which are put upon your shoulders, that even you cannot feel them upon your backs."

Their faith led to deliverance, not immediately but gradually. Even before they were physically freed, the Lord strengthened them to bear their trials, fulfilling His promise in a way they could not have foreseen. Alma's example reminds us that faith isn't always about removing hardships; sometimes, it's about finding strength in God to bear them.

3. Alma the Younger – Faith to Change

Alma the Younger's story is one of powerful transformation. Originally an enemy to the Church, Alma and the sons of Mosiah actively opposed the work of God, causing significant harm to believers. But when an angel appeared, rebuking them with a voice that shook the earth, Alma was so overwhelmed, he lay unconscious, experiencing a vivid, heart-wrenching awareness of his sins.

Alma recounts in Alma 36:17-20 that he cried out to Jesus Christ for mercy, and when he did, he felt a relief so intense that his soul "was filled with joy as exceeding as was [his] pain." Alma's conversion was dramatic, and his faith took root immediately. He became one of the greatest missionaries, devoting his life to preaching the gospel and bringing others to the Savior.

His faith in God's redeeming power was unwavering. Throughout his life, Alma encouraged others to believe in Christ's mercy and to turn from their sins, teaching them that no one was beyond the reach of God's grace. Alma's story teaches us that no matter our past, faith in Christ can transform us, allowing us to become instruments for good.

4. Ammon – Faith to Serve with Courage

Ammon, one of the sons of Mosiah, showed a faith that translated into fearless, selfless service. After his conversion, Ammon dedicated his life to bringing the gospel to the Lamanites, a people who were hostile to the Nephites. Instead of approaching them with the mindset of an enemy, he went with an open heart, willing to serve them in any way. He said, "I desire to dwell among this people for a time, yea, perhaps until the day I die." And then later. "I will be thy servant."

When he was taken in as a servant by King Lamoni, Ammon's faith led him to protect Lamoni's flocks from robbers. The story of Ammon defending the flocks, recounted in Alma 17, demonstrates his courage and his reliance on God. His extraordinary faith earned him the trust and admiration of the king, ultimately opening the door to share the gospel with Lamoni and his people.

Ammon's faith wasn't just belief—it was action. It was a willingness to serve, protect, and love, even at great personal risk. His example reminds us that faith in God often calls us to love and serve others, even those who may not share our beliefs or values. Through Ammon's story, we see how faith and courage can break down barriers, creating opportunities to share the gospel and foster understanding.

5. The Brother of Jared – Faith to See
   God's Hand Clearly

The story of the brother of Jared, found in the book of Ether, is one of the most remarkable accounts of faith in all scripture. As the Jaredites prepared to journey across the ocean, the brother of Jared sought the Lord's guidance in every aspect of their voyage. When he encountered a problem he could not solve—how to have light in their barges —he turned to God with a sincere question, then offered a bold, faith-filled solution: stones that God could touch to give light.

In Ether 3:6, we read that because of the brother of Jared's incredible faith, he was blessed to see the very finger of the Lord touching the stones. His faith was so profound that it allowed him to enter into God's presence. The Lord said to him, "Never has man come before me with such exceeding faith as thou hast."

The brother of Jared's story teaches us the power of coming to God with faith in His abilities, even when our own solutions fall short. His example reminds us that when we approach God with trust and humility, He will guide us, often in ways we cannot imagine. This kind of faith enables us to see His hand in our lives more clearly, just as the brother of Jared did.

6. Joseph Smith – Faith to Seek Truth and Revelation

In modern times, the Prophet Joseph Smith's life is a profound testimony of faith in action. As a young boy, Joseph was confused by the competing religious doctrines of his day and was unsure which church to join. Trusting in the words of James 1:5, he turned to God in prayer, believing that he would receive an answer. His faith brought about one of the most significant events in religious history: the First Vision, in which God the Father and Jesus Christ appeared to him, restoring truth to the earth.

Joseph's life was one of unyielding faith. He faced opposition, betrayal, and persecution, yet he remained committed to the divine work he had been given. In Doctrine and Covenants 122:7, during his time in Liberty Jail, the Lord told Joseph, "All these things shall give thee experience, and shall be for thy good." Joseph's faith helped him endure intense suffering and continue leading the Church, trusting that God's purposes would be fulfilled.

Through Joseph's example, we learn that faith is a journey that requires courage and resilience. His life teaches us that when we turn to God with questions and a sincere desire to know, He will reveal truth and guide us, even if the path is difficult.

7. The Stripling Warriors – Faith to Trust in Promises

In the story of the stripling warriors in the Book of Mormon, we find a group of young men who were taught faith and obedience from their mothers. These young warriors, who had no experience in battle, courageously went to war to defend their people. In Alma 56:47–48, we read, "They had been taught by their mothers, that if they did not doubt, God would deliver them."

The stripling warriors' faith was unwavering. They trusted in the teachings they had received, believing that God would protect them. Remarkably, they fought courageously and none of them perished in battle, fulfilling the promise that had been given them. Their example teaches us that faith is often grounded in the teachings of those who came before us. It reminds us to hold fast to the truths we've learned, to believe in God's promises, and to face challenges with courage.

8. Moroni – Faith to Endure to the End

Moroni, the final prophet in the Book of Mormon, demonstrated a faith that endured even as he faced total isolation. As the last survivor of his people, Moroni witnessed the destruction of his nation and was left to wander alone, recording his final testimony on the golden plates. Despite his isolation, Moroni's faith never wavered.

In Moroni 10:32, he writes, "Yea, come unto Christ, and be perfected in him, and deny yourselves of all ungodliness… then is his grace sufficient for you." Moroni's enduring faith allowed him to focus not on his own suffering but on sharing his final message with future generations.

Moroni's example shows us that faith is not only about beginnings but also about endings. It's about holding on, even when we're alone, and trusting that our efforts will make a difference. His faith-filled endurance is a testament to the strength that comes from complete reliance on the Lord, even when everything else is gone.

Conclusion: A Legacy of Faith

Each of these prophets and leaders faced different challenges, yet their faith was a constant source of strength. Nephi, Alma, Ammon, the brother of Jared, Joseph Smith, the stripling warriors, and Moroni all show us that faith is dynamic. It's what we cling to when we have no clear answers, what drives us to act, and what helps us endure when the way is hard.

Their lives testify of the power of faith to lead us, sustain us, and inspire us. As we read their stories and remember their sacrifices, may we find the courage to follow their example and deepen our faith in God's promises. We, too, can become instruments in His hands, letting faith guide our steps as we strive to live with purpose, courage, and trust in the One who knows the way.

11

FAITH TO MOURN

The plan of happiness involves quite a few not so happy absolutes.

Death being one.

Trailing brightness with them as they go, our loved ones depart and move on to their next place.

And even if we know they are going to a good place, even if we're certain in the belief of a good God, even if death can also include a good amount of peace, it is still just so hard.

And there's the missing, such a sharp sense of loss and wishing to see them again.

My dad was everything people say a good Dad is. But he could never be cliche, not to me.

He was smart and fun and funny.

He asked amazing questions.

He laughed at my jokes.

He helped me be the best me. I really believe I can do anything because of him.

He hoped for our best but in the gentlest way. And he loved me. Man, he loved me. I felt such a loss when he left.

But I couldn't face it.

I visited him the day before he died, and I couldn't face the fact that he was clearly going to die.

I couldn't do it.

I placed my hand on his chest, his body mostly bones, his eyes tired, his voice tired, but his love there in his goodness, in his actions, in his prayers and blessings for us.

I told him I would go but I'll always come back. I told him goodbye in my own way, but I couldn't say the words. I pretended it was not the end.

He placed his hands on my head less than twelve hours before he died, hardly able to stand. But he did it. I felt it was an honor for him.

He stood and blessed my mom and my brother.

He served until the last breath of his life. He died great. He left this world great.

But I couldn't mourn him. I couldn't face his death. I couldn't face his cancer. I couldn't face the suffering, the pain, the starvation of pancreatic cancer. I couldn't face his body wasting away, his emotional health deteriorating with the chemo.

He was so strong. And I couldn't do it. Even now, a year later, the pain is sharp in my throat and my tears are falling. It feels so raw.

Because it takes faith to mourn.

It takes great faith to accept death and to see it as part of the plan and to truly mourn our loved ones.

Can I lose my dad to cancer and still know he is mine? Can I have a firm conviction of the resurrection? Can I have hope in the afterlife and in his happiness?

All of that requires faith.

Faith to mourn.

We join Christ as one who mourned. For He truly bore our sorrows and our grief and with His stripes we are healed.

"Blessed are those who mourn for they shall be comforted."

The acceptance of sorrow, of the cause of sorrow and a trust in God's love and His plan lead to great blessings of comfort and peace and understanding.

Jesus mourned. He wept. He sorrowed. It places us in a position of understanding and empathy and godlike love for others.

When my Dad was first diagnosed, and we all knew he was going to die, a friend approached at church and cried for me, which of course made me cry with her. And I love her for that.

Mourning changes us.

We become something a bit more holy ourselves.

And we gain the ability to mourn with others, to feel their sorrow with them, to participate in that holiness together.

I'm still missing my Dad. I'm still crying over him. And I'm still loving him. My path of mourning has been gradual and gentle and what I could bear.

But as I allow myself to mourn, I feel closer to him than I ever have. I feel closer to Christ than before, and I know more about myself and our purpose here on Earth.

The faith to mourn is a hard bridge to cross, but in my mourning, my love is sweeter, my faith is stronger, and peace is available. Mourning my dad will always be a part of me. I'll always miss him. I'll always feel sad. But there is a holiness that will also always be there, a sacred closeness that can only be gained through mourning someone you love as much as I love him.

12

STRENGTHENING FAITH AMID MENTAL ILLNESS

When I was recovering from COVID in the hospital, I felt numb. And I felt exhausted. And for some reason, reaching out to God felt impossible.

I couldn't feel Him.

And that was scary.

I called my husband and told him to pray for me because I really felt like his prayers would be heard and mine were stopping in the hospital room.

But as with all scary hard things, I learned something.

While laying there totally isolated in my room, I was reminded of the logical, true, emotionless things that I know.

One of those is that I had received lots of answers to prayers.

I had always felt close to God.

I knew He was out there.

Not *feeling* close, didn't mean he *wasn't* close.

And I decided that I could move forward in faith without feelings, without emotion, that memories and thoughts could be enough.

Even though I couldn't feel answers to prayer nor could I feel like anyone was listening, in my mind I knew all those things had happened before. I knew I had a relationship with God. I knew He heard my prayers. Logically and mentally, without any feelings in my heart, I knew that prayer worked.

Relying mentally on something that I used to feel emotionally helped me to hold on through what was initially a scary sensation.

I have since felt a great amount of empathy for those of us who have bouts of depression or sadness or weakness, who feel like they can't pray or that even if they could, they wouldn't be able to feel close to God.

I collected some ideas of ways we can still keep moving forward with faith even if we aren't feeling the power of our faith in the moment. Here are a few of the ideas:

1. Engage in Prayer and Meditation

Prayer and meditation serve as bridges to God, offering moments of peace and connection even amidst turmoil. While feelings of closeness to God may ebb, the act of prayer itself demonstrates faith. It creates a habit. It builds on itself and strengthens us. Prayer doesn't have to be an emotional experience to be real and connecting to God. In moments of struggle:

Focus on honesty in prayer: Express doubts, fears, and pain openly to God. Scriptures like Psalm 34:18 remind us, "The Lord is close to the brokenhearted and saves those who are crushed in spirit." And also express gratitude, love, praise and acknowledgement of the goodness in life.

Incorporate meditative practices: Meditation on sacred passages or quiet reflection on God's presence can provide calm. Even brief, focused breathing with the repetition of a comforting phrase, such as "Be still and know that I am God" (Psalm 46:10), can center the mind.

Create a routine: Consistency in prayer, even when emotions feel numb, reinforces a commitment to faith. Set aside specific times each day to pray or meditate, turning it into a habit rather than relying on fluctuating feelings.

Over time, these practices can foster a sense of stability and reinforce the truth of God's presence, even when it feels distant.

2. Seek Support from Faith Communities

Isolation is a common struggle during mental health challenges, yet engaging with others in faith-based settings can provide much-needed connection and encouragement. Faith communities offer:

> A sense of belonging: Attending services, participating in small groups, or joining prayer circles can help individuals feel seen and supported.
>
> Encouragement from shared experiences: Hearing stories of others who have faced trials and maintained their faith can inspire resilience. In Hebrews 10:24-25, believers are urged to "spur one another on toward love and good deeds" and "not give up meeting together."
>
> Opportunities for accountability: Trusted community members can offer reminders of God's promises and encouragement to stay grounded in faith practices.

Even when participation feels daunting, small steps —such as attending a service or reaching out to someone, anyone—can open doors to renewed strength and companionship.

3. Study Sacred Texts

Scriptures often address the complexities of human suffering, offering wisdom and reassurance. We can find a roadmap for enduring difficult seasons. Almost every prophet in the scriptures endured difficult trials.

Focus on passages about perseverance: Verses like James 1:2-4, which speaks of trials producing perseverance, can offer hope that struggles have purpose.

Reflect on stories of faith in adversity: The Bible recounts the trials of Job, David, and others who faced immense challenges yet clung to God. Their stories can resonate deeply with personal experiences of struggle.

Memorize uplifting verses: Having scripture readily available in memory can serve as an anchor during moments of anxiety or despair.

Approach scripture study with patience, allowing its truths to sink in over time. Pairing study with journaling or discussion can deepen understanding and make the process more engaging.

4. Serve Others

Helping others, even in small ways, shifts focus

from internal struggles to external needs, creating opportunities for renewed purpose and connection.

> Volunteer within your community: Simple acts of kindness—delivering meals, assisting at a shelter, or participating in church outreach programs —demonstrate God's love in action.
>
> Offer emotional support to others: Sometimes, being present for someone else facing difficulty can foster mutual healing. Galatians 6:2 encourages believers to "carry each other's burdens, and in this way you will fulfill the law of Christ."
>
> Recognize the spiritual benefits of service: Serving others often leads to gratitude and a deeper sense of connection with God's work in the world.

Engaging in acts of service reminds us of our capacity to make a difference, even during personal hardship.

5. Seek Professional Help

Mental health struggles often require professional intervention, and integrating faith into this process can be profoundly healing.

Find a faith-sensitive therapist: Many counselors incorporate spiritual beliefs into therapy, helping clients navigate mental health challenges without compromising their faith.

Embrace the intersection of science and faith: Utilizing therapy or medication does not diminish reliance on God but acknowledges that healing can come through various means.

Seeking help is an act of courage and faith in itself, reflecting trust in God's provision through others.

6. Practice Gratitude

Mental illness often narrows focus to negative thoughts and emotions, making it difficult to recognize blessings. Practicing gratitude can shift this perspective, creating space for hope and renewed faith.

Start a gratitude journal: Write down three things each day, no matter how small, for which you are thankful. Over time, this practice reinforces a habit of noticing God's provision.

Reflect on past faithfulness: Remembering times when God provided strength or guidance in the past can build confidence in His presence during current struggles.

Focus on simple joys: A sunrise, a kind word, or a comforting meal can be reminders of God's care.

Gratitude doesn't dismiss pain but reframes it within a broader context of God's ongoing goodness.

7. Navigate Doubt and Rebuild Trust

It's natural to experience doubt or frustration with God during times of mental illness. Faith is not a static state but a journey, marked by both struggle and growth. To navigate these challenges:

Acknowledge your feelings: Allow yourself to question and grieve without guilt. God's love is not contingent on unwavering belief.

Seek counsel from trusted mentors: Faith leaders or spiritual friends can provide guidance and reassurance. Seek trusted sources for learning and growth. Focus on faith filled paths and stay away from those which fuel your doubt.

Rest in God's grace: Remember that faith is ultimately a gift, sustained by God's grace and seen in our action and effort.

Over time, faith can be rebuilt, even if it looks different from before.

Conclusion: Holding On When Feelings Falter

Faith during mental illness often requires leaning on what you know to be true, even when it cannot be felt in the heart. Practices such as prayer, community engagement, scripture study, and professional support provide a foundation for navigating the valleys of mental health struggles. We can find renewed strength, purpose, and connection to God's unchanging presence.

Remember, faith is not measured by the absence of struggle but by the willingness to seek God amid it. As Psalm 23 reminds us, "Even though I walk through the valley of the shadow of death, I will fear no evil, for thou art with me." Remember that in Christ's final moments, He called out, asking why His father had deserted Him. He too felt alone. But He was not. He could no longer feel the presence of His father, but God never stopped loving Him, never gave up on Him and was always there. We are never really alone even if we feel like we are. Trusting in this truth, even when God feels distant, is a profound act of faith.

13

TO KNOW GOD IS TO LOVE
AND TRUST HIM

The more we know Christ, the greater our ability to have faith in Him.

I am on a quest to know Him.

Peter knew Him. What did Peter know about the Savior that made him think he could walk on water?

Our faith grows with our knowledge.

That seems different than we normally think about faith. Isn't faith believing without seeing, the precursor to knowledge?

But we can't really have faith in Christ without knowing Him. The more we know, the more we love, trust, and have faith in Jesus Christ. Isn't that incredible? The more we know, the more we love and trust.

I think knowing Christ comes from learning and doing. The times I feel closest to Him have been in the midst of consistent scripture study and consistent service for Him.

There is a lot we can learn about Him.

We can study His attributes. We can emulate them. The more we become like Him, the better we know Him.

Consider a few of the following attributes of Christ as traits to focus our own growth. As we try to be more like Him, we understand Him better.

Divine Love

Central to Christ's character is His perfect, unconditional love for all of God's children. This love, often referred to as charity, is the foundation of His mission and ministry. The Book of Mormon describes charity as "the pure love of Christ" (Moroni 7:47; 1 Corinthians 13). His love is evident in every act of His life, from healing the sick to forgiving His persecutors.

He cried with his friends, fed thousands, taught others, cared for his mother, served, helped, loved.

The epitome of Christ's love is found in the Atonement. As recorded in the New Testament, Christ willingly suffered for the sins and pains of all humanity in the Garden of Gethsemane and on the cross (Luke 22:44; Matthew 27:46). This ultimate act of love ensures that all who repent and follow Him can receive forgiveness and eternal life. His love is personal, encompassing every individual. President Thomas S. Monson, a former prophet of The Church of Jesus Christ of Latter Day Saints, emphasized this when he said, "His love is there for you whether or not you feel you deserve love."

Humility

Christ's humility is demonstrated in His willingness to submit entirely to the will of the Father. In the pre-mortal existence, He accepted the role of Redeemer, declaring, "Here am I, send me" (Abraham 3:27). During His mortal ministry, He consistently deferred glory to His Father, saying, "I seek not mine own will, but the will of the Father which hath sent me" (John 5:30).

His humility is also evident in the circumstances of His birth. Born in a lowly stable and laid in a manger, Christ came into the world in the humblest of settings (Luke 2:7). Even as the King of Kings, He washed the feet of His disciples, teaching that true greatness comes through service (John 13:4–15).

Humility is a precursor to any other growth and essential for us to exercise any sort of power to help others. It enables us to see God's hand more freely and to feel gratitude and love for Him as a result.

Obedience

Jesus Christ's perfect obedience to God the Father underscores His sinless life and divine mission. He declared, "I do always those things that please [the Father]" (John 8:29). This unwavering obedience was most profoundly demonstrated in the Garden of Gethsemane, where He prayed, "Not my will, but thine, be done" (Luke 22:42).

He marked the path so clearly when he chose to be baptized even without a single sin. He certainly showed that obedience is the choice even when you don't completely understand the purpose. God immediately praised His son from heaven saying, "This is my beloved son, in whom I am well pleased."

For us, obedience is not a constraint but a pathway to freedom, allowing individuals to feel closer to God and to become more like the Savior and receive the blessings of the gospel.

Compassion

The Savior's compassion is woven throughout His ministry. He consistently showed mercy to those who were marginalized, afflicted, or despised. In the New Testament, we read of His healing of the sick, raising of the dead, and feeding of the multitudes. One moving example is His interaction with the woman taken in adultery. Rather than condemn her, Christ extended mercy, saying, "Neither do I condemn thee: go, and sin no more" (John 8:11). He cried with those who were so desperately missing Lazarus. He healed and ministered to those no one else saw.

In the Book of Mormon, Christ's compassion is powerfully illustrated during His appearance to the Nephites. After teaching and blessing them, He perceived their sorrow and remained with them longer, healing their sick and praying for them (3 Nephi 17:5–9). This tender ministry reveals His deep empathy and love for all.

Patience

Patience is another hallmark of Christ's character. Throughout His ministry, He bore persecution, misunderstanding, and rejection with calm endurance. When reviled, He "reviled not again" (1 Peter 2:23). Even in His suffering, He forgave His executioners, saying, "Father, forgive them; for they know not what they do" (Luke 23:34).

There was a time when wherever He walked, people followed, thousands at a time and many were hungry. They sought Him for reasons other than the incredible doctrine that He taught. He healed them. He fed them.

Wisdom

Jesus Christ's wisdom is unparalleled. His teachings, whether delivered through parables or direct instruction, reveal profound spiritual truths. The Sermon on the Mount, recorded in Matthew 5–7, is a masterful discourse on righteous living, touching on topics such as forgiveness, love, and the pure in heart. From a young age he was found speaking with Rabbis in the temple hearing and answering their questions. He was well read and a dedicated student of the scriptures.

One notable example of His wisdom is His response to the Pharisees' attempt to trap Him with a question about paying taxes to Caesar. Christ's reply, "Render therefore unto Caesar the things which are Caesar's; and unto God the things that are God's" (Matthew 22:21), not only silenced His critics but also provided an enduring principle about balancing earthly responsibilities with spiritual priorities.

Power

Christ's power is divine. He is all powerful. As the creator, the Earth moves according to His will. With just three words, "I am He." The Roman soldiers fell back in His presence. His miracles, such as calming the storm, healing the sick, and raising the dead, testify of His authority over nature and life. The withered fig tree showed his followers that he has power over life and death, that He could have avoided the crucifixion if he chose. His ultimate demonstration of power was His victory over sin and death through the Atonement and Resurrection.

In the Book of Mormon, Abinadi teaches about Christ's power, declaring, "He is the light and the life of the world; yea, a light that is endless, that can never be darkened" (Mosiah 16:9). His power is not only infinite but also available to all who exercise faith in Him.

As grand and vast as his power is, it is also evident in highly personal ways in each of our lives. We rely on Christ's power to overcome personal weaknesses, resist temptation, and endure challenges. Through His grace, they can be strengthened and ultimately achieve eternal life.

As we immerse ourselves in the scriptures, we come to know Jesus Christ more intimately. The Bible and the Book of Mormon complement each other, each offering unique insights into His divine character and mission. Together, they testify of His compassion, wisdom, humility, power, and love.

The more we know Him through the scriptures, the more we try to follow Him and act as He did or would, the stronger our Faith in Him.

And who is He? Who is Christ?

What kind of person was he, walking on the earth? Did he laugh and play and work and converse and feel sad and happy and all the things we do?

What did He enjoy? What makes Him happy? What makes Him sorrow?

Get to know Him. He reveals Himself to each of us in personal, unique ways that are best suited to our understanding. He is everything we read that He is and more. And he loves us with a kind of love that covers all, in spite of all, and never ever fails. No matter what, He will help us along if that is what we want.

And then as we learn about Him, we start doing.

Do all the things we know He would do.

Reach out. Love. Help. Work.

It is in the doing and the acting that we will walk with him at our side. We will be engaged with Him in doing great things. We will come to know Him.

I have felt Him at my side symbolically and maybe even literally. Some of my most sacred moments were shared with Him, and all of them involved working and doing and acting and walking in Faith as I tried to walk at His side, doing His work.

I hope it is evident in my words of my great love and respect for Him. I so wish to be a good disciple, and I fail so often. But to some degree, I know Him, and I know He loves me. And that is the greatest blessing of my life.

14

BE STILL AND KNOW

We have heard that the wise man builds his house on a rock so when the rains come and floods rise, his house is immovable, firm and steadfast.

"The House on the rock stood still."

All-important words.

I have recently been keyed into the idea that being still is related to firm foundations and a surety during a storm.

"Be Still and Know that I am God."

When the storms were scaring even seasoned fishermen and Jesus slept in the back of the boat…

He was awakened.

He calmed the storm with the words, "Be Still."

The winds and the waves obeyed.

But could there have been more to his message? Was he speaking to more than just the storm and sea?

Could he also be commanding the hearts and the faith of his followers? Be still. Be sure. Be steadfast. Be immovable.

And know that I am God.

When He calmed the storm, their first response was "Surely though art the son of God." They were still, and they knew. The same pattern. Be still and know.

I used to think that being still was a calm meditative state in a beautiful garden with the sound of falling water.

Perhaps this type of stillness contributes to our sureness in Christ.

But I think the command to be still perhaps leans more toward the idea of an unwavering faith amid the storm—

When there is absolute chaos all around, and we are sure and steadfast in Christ.

I think that is a bit more realistic than attempting to find calm and peaceful surroundings all the time.

Be immovable. Hold on during the storm.

But I think it also means to take time for stillness.

Let our minds wander, let our thoughts focus in on important things.

Listen.

Feel.

Be.

And it would help if it was quiet. Don't let the world drown out our priorities or our focus.

I'm sure that being still also means to physically still our minds and bodies and exert mental focus to work on important things. The mental exercise to singularly focus takes practice and stamina.

Stillness can mean the singular focus and stillness of mind that is required to do mental work.

Still is also sure.

Still is unmoving and unwavering.

Still is eternal.

And our stillness in Christ helps us to know Him.

A foundation built on Christ will not fall.

A foundation on Him means that no matter what is going on around us, we are unmoved in our faith in Christ. Sure of His love. Faithful in His commands.

The command to 'be still and know that I am God' was given amidst some of the worst persecution the early pioneer saints had ever faced. They were mobbed, crops destroyed, homes ransacked, property ruined, injured by others.

They were threatened and being forced to leave Missouri, which at the time was considered the promised land for them. It was meant to be the place where they would dwell in peace.

There was no sense of outward stillness, no waterfalls, no peaceful surroundings. It was chaos, loneliness, persecution, horror. And yet the command, "…Let your hearts be comforted concerning Zion, for all flesh is in my hands. Be still and know that I am God."

The Saints were not still at the time.

Some were contentious, disruptive, and disobedient.

Was the command meant to comfort those who were righteous, letting them know they could be at peace?

And at the same time was it meant to be instructive to those who were causing trouble, as a reminder to be still, be sure, return to the path and the foundation on which they should be built?

Whatever the purpose, it shows that being still has little to do with the circumstances of our lives. Being still can happen no matter what is going on around us.

Great demonstrations of God's power can be seen in moments of unrest, fear, and lack of peace.

Remain sure during the storm, and you will see God's hand.

Be still and His power will be revealed.

Be still and all will become clear.

I can almost see it meaning, to "hang in there with your faith." Keep holding to your belief.

The storm will pass and somewhere in all this will be some amazing evidence of God's hand in your life. You will know that He. Is. God.

Be still.

In the scariest, darkest moments of your life will come the greatest test of your stillness.

In the challenging times of Christ's ministry, some of His followers stopped following.

He asked his disciples, "Will ye also go away?"

We may struggle, we may wish to go away. We may even do so for a time. But ever present, ever watchful ever ready will always be our Savior.

To the question, "Will ye also go away?" We can answer, "To whom would we go. Thou art the Christ."

Look to Him for your stillness, for your sure foundation, and know that He. Is. God.

15

FAITH IN CHRIST

The faith to walk.

The faith to do, to be, to love, to move, to create, to let go—that faith, is an action kind of faith.

And it all stems from the stillness and the assurance in our Savior Jesus Christ.

We have faith in all kinds of things, in the plan, the gospel way of living, families being eternal.

We have faith every day.

In many important things.

We have faith in a gospel and in a church that provides a way to return to God one day.

But the reason, the purpose, the joy behind it all begins and ends with our faith in Jesus Christ.

Our faith in Him began long before we came to earth even.

We knew Him, and when He said He would come to earth and Atone for our sins, die and live again, we believed Him.

We trusted He would do what He said he would do.

Not just trusted, we banked everything on Him.

We left our home with God, knowing we might not return, knowing we were going to a tough hard place, knowing it was also amazingly wonderful and full of joy.

We agreed to come on the promise from Him that He would do His part. He said, "Here am I, send me." And we were IN!

Our faith in Him is sure. Even if we can't remember, it is sure. Or we wouldn't be here. We demonstrated faith and trust in the Lord before we came, and we are doing it again every single day.

Separate from Christ, daily functions require faith or at least a belief in others.

We recently had a contractor lie to us on several occasions. His unapologetic dishonesty about many things stirred my awareness that we rely on and function on a belief in the honesty of others. That system gives space for a great many disappointments and a loss of trust in others. We have all undoubtedly been disappointed in others at one point or another. We have all undoubtedly been the cause of disappointment.

But though all men and women might fail us at one point or another, our God never will.

Jesus Christ is the way, the truth and the life. He is the means by which we can return to that place we loved and left, to the side of our Heavenly Father. He's the reason we agreed to go, and he's the reason we will once again return.

And now that we have arrived and are living this life of growth and becoming and struggle and trial and mistakes and sickness and everything hard and good and also joyful and glorious, He is the reason we can keep going.

Our faith in Him is the most motivating, strengthening force we have.

Think about all of your whys.

Why do you do hard things?

Why do you get up every day?

Why are you YOU?

My biggest and greatest and surest why is Him.

Sometimes that faith is tested.

Do I love all the different trials that come my way?

Do I want to forgive mean ugly people who are unrepentant?

Faith in Christ is the reason to do hard things anyway.

Are His commandments challenging sometimes?

Faith in Christ is the reason to obey.

Are we tired and wish to step away to a life of ease?

Faith in Christ is the reason to keep working and loving.

And indeed there are trials that hit us so hard, they steal our breath, tighten our throats, disrupt our sleep, test our patience, and break our hearts. But we keep going because He is our strength and our song and our salvation. We can because of Him.

We fail sometimes, lots of times.

We make so many mistakes it's overwhelming.

We are not perfect and can't be perfect in this life nor could we be alone.

In fact, we were meant to make mistakes: to try, fail, try again, learn, become.

We were meant to be presented with tough choices, nuanced truths, conflicting good things, and have to figure out our way.

That is how to learn, and we were meant to learn.

The path to Christ, the way of Faith in Him is simple.

"If ye love me, keep my commandments."

And the growth is huge, because on that path live a million options and a hundred stumbling blocks, distractions, good and bad, and choices.

All the choices.

But our faith in Christ will carry us.

And one day, we will see Him as He is.

We will know Him.

The nature of Christ.

The kind one, the loving one, the obedient one, the diligent one, the trustworthy one, the one without fault. The brilliant all-knowing all powerful one. The patient one.

The one.

I Am.

The great son of God, the creator, the king, our tender humble, immensely strong Savior and Redeemer, Jesus Christ.

He is sure and deserving of our trust. Our faith in Him grows brighter and brighter until the perfect day, the day when He comes again—The brightest of all days when He descends from the East like the sun, because He is the son.

The Great Creator will return again to His creation.

We will see Him as He is, and we will know Him and love Him.

And in that day, our faith in Him will be sure.

Until then, let us walk. Let us have the faith to walk every day better and brighter.

Friends. I hope something in these reflections brought you closer to Jesus Christ. I hope you know He is ever ready and always there. His love transcends everything. Turn to Him. Love Him back. Follow Him. Walk. And keeping walking. Walk to Him literally, kneel at His feet and fall into His embrace.

In His name, Amen.

ACKNOWLEDGMENTS

So much love went into this book. And so many kind friends' eyes and thoughts.

Thank you to Anneka Walker and Sarah L. McConkie for your early look at my pages. Your beautiful mark is seen here.

Thank you for a later look from Krista Isaacson who I trust completely with this kind of project.

And many thanks to my husband Dustin who always wonders how errors fight their way through many edits. I gave him the last look so maybe once and for all they will be eradicated. All joking aside. He has the best eye of anyone I've seen. Many thanks to him. For everything.

Most of all I really do thank our Lord and Savior, Jesus Christ. We were asked recently if we believed in Christ's divinity or if He was a prophet to us. I hope the book answers that question, but just in case:

I believe in Christ as the Creator of the world

and my Savior and Redeemer, as the only way, truth and life and the reason I will ever be able to return to Heaven one day. He is God. He lived, died for us and was resurrected. He lives again! I love Him with all my heart and thank Him for His endless patience and help and for assisting me in being able to create anything at all, but most especially this book.

It was likely better for me to write it than for any person who will read its pages.

With great love and thanks,

Jen

ABOUT THE AUTHOR

Hello. I'm Jen.

I wish we were sitting across the table at lunch or lounging together on a soft deep couch. These kinds of conversations always go better in person. And besides, I'd love to hear what you have to say too.

But instead, you'll find a stream of consciousness in these pages—my thoughts on the Faith it takes to do so many different things. And if my thoughts ignite your thoughts and you want to share them with me, I'd be thrilled to listen. http://www.jengeiglejohnson.com

I have written a whole bunch of fiction, and I love the power of stories.

Life has taught me any number of things. Just like it's taught you.

I decided to make my thoughts available to more people in case something in here could give you a little boost, strengthen your Faith, or help you see God in your life.

I chose not to seek publication through a publisher. There is no middle man. This is just me and you and transparency and all of us trying to do our best.

The book will come in small edible portions. You can read it all at once or bit by bit.

It's fun sized!

Thank you for taking a chance on this solo project of mine.

And as always, thank you for reading.

Jen Geigle Johnson

FOLLOW JEN

Some of Jen's other published books
Like Unto Moroni

The Duke's Second Chance
The Earl's Winning Wager
Her Lady's Whims and Whimsies
Suitors for the Proper Miss
Pining for Lord Lockhart
The Foibles and Follies of Miss Grace

The Nobleman's Daughter
Two lovers in disguise

Scarlet
The Pimpernel retold

A Lady's Maid
Can she love again?

His Lady in Hiding
Hiding out as his maid.

A Foreign Crown
Trilogy of Regency Royals

Spun of Gold
Rumpelstilskin Retold

Dating the Duke
Time Travel: Regency man in NYC

Charmed by His Lordship
The antics of a fake friendship

Tabitha's Folly
Four over-protective brothers

To read Damen's Secret
The Villain's Romance

Follow her Newsletter

www.ingramcontent.com/pod-product-compliance
Lightning Source LLC
Chambersburg PA
CBHW032035040426
42449CB00007B/898